Transforming College Teaching Evaluation

Transforming College Teaching Evaluation

A Framework for Advancing Instructional Excellence

ANN E. AUSTIN
NOAH D. FINKELSTEIN
ANDREA FOLLMER GREENHOOT
DOUG WARD
GABRIELA CORNEJO WEAVER

Harvard Education Press
Cambridge, Massachusetts

Paperback ISBN 9798895570159

Library of Congress Cataloging-in-Publication Data is on file.

Published by Harvard Education Press,
an imprint of the Harvard Education Publishing Group

Harvard Education Press
8 Story Street
Cambridge, MA 02138

Cover Design: Patrick Ciano
Cover Image: Margi via Getty Images

The typefaces in this book are Carrara and Gotham.

To the many educators in colleges and universities who dedicate their efforts, energy, and ideas to preparing the full array of learners for meaningful, engaging, and productive lives.

CONTENTS

FOREWORD

THIS IS A MOMENT OF ENORMITY for higher education—one that lends a new sense of urgency to democratizing opportunity through the transformative power of teaching excellence in the classroom and beyond. Once considered a cornerstone of the American dream, burgeoning skepticism has arisen around the value of a college degree, with concerns ranging from the contention that higher education is too expensive and too difficult to access to accusations that colleges and universities are failing to prepare students with the skills necessary for a twenty-first-century workforce. These changing attitudes have opened the door and created a new permission structure for infringements upon academic freedom and institutional autonomy in the form of federal and state legislation circumscribing who gets admitted to colleges and universities, what is taught, how it is taught, and by whom.

The challenges posed for faculty—particularly VITAL faculty (visiting instructors, temporary, adjunct, and lecturers)—arising from this societal shift are profound in their nature and scope. Yet the problems themselves are nothing new. For decades, the demands of an increasingly competitive climate in academia have precipitated faculty burnout and exhaustion, which have now reached epidemic proportions.[1] And it has always been the case that certain faculty, especially women and faculty of color, have exceeded the level of work outlined in their job descriptions by engaging in unrecognized service, often at the expense of their research, and by providing outstanding mentorship—work recently made more visible by studies indicating that students are becoming increasingly disengaged in the classroom, and anxiety, depression, and despair have surpassed financial considerations as the primary reason students are either dropping out of college or not attending in the first place.[2] Faculty members across all disciplines have endeavored to fulfill their professional responsibilities by cultivating meaningful discussion and fostering mutually respectful debate among students, tasks made more complicated by a political climate fomenting fear around addressing controversial topics in order to avoid professional repercussions. Moreover, heavy workloads, a strong sense of responsibility to their students and the profession, and unrelenting pressure to publish are longstanding factors contributing to the inability of faculty to disconnect from their work. Even so, the rapid pace of technological advancement isn't helping; faculty are ostensibly on call at all times and are now charged with the monumental job of helping students adapt in a new era of AI and human thinking.

As these responsibilities are thrown into greater relief, it has become clear that when it comes to evaluating faculty, existing measures are inadequate for capturing the breadth, depth, and expansiveness of their contributions. High-stakes standardized teaching evaluation instruments (i.e., student ratings), introduced in the 1920s, continue to be used at institutions across the country for tenure, reappointment, and promotion decisions, despite shortcomings related to proven racial, gender, and ethnic biases; inconsistent criteria; frequent lack of correspondence to learning outcomes; and low online response rates, with results often correlating to the assigned grade.[3] By providing a comprehensive framework for a more holistic, equitable approach to the evaluation of teaching, aligned with evidence-based, effective, and inclusive teaching practice, the authors of *Transforming College Teaching Evaluation: A Framework for Advancing Instructional Excellence* invite a reimagining of how teaching should be assessed and how faculty should be supported in the classroom. They simultaneously issue a call to action to engage in the institutional transformation necessary to strengthen faculty practices and enhance the culture of teaching and learning at colleges and universities of all types.

Among the book's most valuable assets is the introduction of an evidence-based framework for nurturing institutional cultures that elevate the teaching mission and promote excellence in teaching and learning at every level. This framework is centered on a multifaceted rubric, TEval, whose seven dimensions are designed to capture the totality of teaching practice. In addition to defining expectations and incorporating guiding questions, the framework also helps illuminate sources of evidence grounded in the authors' trailblazing NSF-funded research on advancing STEM undergraduate education. The findings from this research offer insights into successfully navigating the intricacies of change management in relation to the reform of teaching evaluations. The TEval rubric and dynamic case studies are designed to prompt faculty to reflect upon and discuss the principles, values, and purposes informing their teaching and to encourage faculty and administrative changemakers to revolutionize and reinvigorate the learning community by recognizing, articulating, and valuing the many dimensions involved in teaching excellence.

Yet it is work that acknowledges the critical role of faculty autonomy and shared governance, as well as departmental and institutional cultures, in advancing organizational change. As a result, the case studies drawn from the authors' own experiences in different departments at their home institutions serve as a backdrop and practical guide for an application of the framework to readers' unique circumstances and diverse disciplinary contexts. The innovative system advanced by the authors empowers faculty members to continually revisit the question of why they are asking students to do what is required in their classrooms and then allows them to provide context and document the changes they have adopted for learning improvement. It is one that positions teaching evaluations as a critical tool for learning, facilitates student engagement, and aims to counteract biases by utilizing a variety of perspectives and forms of evidence.

This book puts forward a compelling rationale for a systemic approach to transforming teaching evaluations. In the process, it demonstrates the ways in which increased transparency around the value proposition of teaching excellence, combined with the support and recognition of faculty who embrace improved teaching practices, will result in more inclusive and equitable classroom environments for students and faculty alike. In the end, the guidance and recommendations championed by the authors as catalysts for institutional change are indispensable for fulfilling the promises higher education has made to our students and to our society, ensuring that all students are positioned for success in work, citizenship, and life and that faculty are thriving in their teaching careers, even as they continue to lead in research and service to the community.

Lynn Pasquerella
President, American Association of Colleges and Universities

Introduction

Transforming Teaching Evaluation: A Time for Change

UNIVERSITIES AND COLLEGES ACROSS the United States are committing to more effective, inclusive, and equitable approaches to learning and nurturing institutional cultures to more fully value teaching. Effective approaches to teaching evaluation have the potential to bolster that process by improving the quality of teaching and learning practices. Often, however, institutional approaches to evaluation do not recognize the many dimensions involved in effective teaching, enable biases that undermine excellence in education, and fail to encourage conversations and institutional cultures that value learning. The purpose of this book is to advance efforts to improve teaching evaluation in ways that strengthen teaching and learning processes, enrich faculty practice, and enhance an institution's culture of teaching and learning.

This book responds to the accelerating interest in excellence in teaching in higher education. We provide a framework for a holistic approach to teaching evaluation, accompanied by descriptions of a rubric to guide teaching evaluation and practical processes and strategies for engaging faculty in this work. It shows how robust teaching evaluation can make visible the many aspects of teaching practice that are critically important but often overlooked and that contribute to better student learning. Institutional leaders will find guidance and recommendations for how to change teaching evaluation within departments and at the institutional level. The lessons for practice are supported by the authors' experiences in facilitating transformation of teaching evaluation at three universities and the related research in which they have engaged to develop lessons about the process of improving teaching evaluation—essentially, an organizational change endeavor.

WHY IS REFORM OF TEACHING EVALUATION IMPORTANT AT THIS TIME?

The need for better approaches to teaching evaluation has been percolating for years.[1] The recent surge of interest is associated with a combination of factors, including the pressing need for universities to place greater emphasis on learning and equitable student success, widespread recognition of the limitations of student surveys, and a need to support the breadth of work carried out by the growing number of contingent, or VITAL (visiting instructional, temporary, adjunct, and lecturing) faculty, who are deeply involved with higher education's teaching mission.[2] Universities and colleges face strong pressures to improve learning, increase student success, and ensure that financial investments in higher education result in graduates prepared to enter the workforce. Dramatically rising costs have added to political pressures for universities to demonstrate their value in providing effective teaching, especially as many students leave college deeply in debt but without a clear path to employment or, in some cases, without a degree. Universities are pressed to find ways to encourage student success for increasingly diverse populations of students rather than just weeding out those who cannot pass high-stakes exams. Collectively, these conditions create a high need for wider use of evidence-based teaching practices. These include active engagement in learning processes, peer-to-peer interactions, problem-based learning, research experiences, and frequent, targeted feedback on both progress in learning and areas needing improvement.[3] These methods have been shown to enhance student learning and success, and will better prepare all students to lead meaningful and impactful lives as citizens, members of the workforce, and contributors to a dynamic, rapidly changing world. Although decades of research on improving undergraduate education have led to significant changes in teaching practices, the persistence of didactic teaching and systemic inequities in student outcomes, especially in STEM education, indicate that much work remains to ensure successful learning outcomes for all students.[4]

One way to elevate the importance of the teaching mission is to provide explicit support and reward for faculty who embrace better practices. Organizational reward and recognition systems convey messages about what is valued, and therefore, where faculty members should focus their efforts and time. However, if faculty are to invest time in improving courses and supporting student learning using evidence-based, inclusive practices, this work must be appropriately recognized and rewarded. Rewarding effective teaching requires evaluation methods that align with those practices. Furthermore, in an era where faculty may experience burnout from an excessive array of demands, thoughtful discussion about teaching evaluation among colleagues can provide avenues for clarifying and reaching reasonable expectations that align with institutional priorities—thus ensuring that faculty work in support of those expectations is valued, recognized, and rewarded.[5] Externalizing expectations of faculty practice through this reformed evaluation and reward system can also provide a mechanism for institutions to consider how to review the overall portfolio of work required of faculty, what to include and emphasize, and what to remove from the ever-growing sets of expectations.

While robust evaluation processes would be useful in sending messages about institutional priorities around teaching excellence, the usual teaching evaluation processes have many shortcomings. The most commonly used systems to document and evaluate teaching overlook and undervalue the intellectual work of effective and inclusive teaching and the care that excellent instructors put into creating inclusive and motivating learning climates.[6] Most universities and departments heavily rely on scores from student surveys and to a lesser degree on single, "drive-by" class visits by peers who then write letters that often emphasize instructor knowledge and presentation of material.[7] These surface-level methods focus on a narrow range of teaching practices, provide minimal feedback to improve teaching, and do little to reward faculty for the substantial intellectual work involved in reflective and effective teaching. Student surveys of teaching are unreliable indicators of how effectively instruction promotes actual learning outcomes. Furthermore, they have been shown to be susceptible to multiple forms of bias.[8] Research shows that student ratings of teaching are associated with a variety of factors, such as instructor leniency in grading, the level of difficulty and amount of work in a course, and instructors' gender, race, or ethnicity. Faculty are often penalized with lower scores when they attempt to implement evidence-based teaching strategies, even when those strategies lead to better student outcomes.[9] Poor response rates after a widespread shift to online surveys have further diminished their validity.[10] Furthermore, nonwhite faculty and those for whom English is not the first language tend to receive lower evaluations from students than their white and first-language English-speaking colleagues.[11] Although the evidence is less consistent, female instructors tend to receive lower ratings than their male counterparts.[12] This array of concerns highlights that teaching evaluation reform is in need of significant attention.

Reform in teaching evaluation can bring recognition to the wide array of work that is involved in effective teaching, including developing curriculum, identifying and creating course materials, scaffolding learning, assessing learning outcomes, providing feedback, and engaging in course revision. Discussions of teaching evaluation can also help faculty create more inclusive, equitable learning contexts, and reduce the impact of implicit bias in classrooms. Our work has shown that when faculty members consider ways to change the evaluation of teaching, a conversation initially focused on the logistics of evaluation often moves to how learning occurs in a specific field and how teaching can more fully support learning for the full array of students. Evaluation processes that are more comprehensive, holistic, and valid are needed to drive adoption of educational practices that increase student success, more equitably recognize and reward faculty investment in such practices, and elevate consideration of teaching quality in faculty reward systems.

Many universities and colleges are interested in finding a better approach to evaluating teaching that addresses these concerns. The COVID-19 pandemic provided an opening to encourage this interest and solidify efforts to embrace a more substantial, holistic system of evaluation that encourages and supports continual improvement in teaching. During the pandemic, many instructors devoted countless unpaid hours to adapting their courses for online instruction, learning new technologies and new modes of interacting with students, and continually following up with students who lost the daily structure of their lives and struggled to stay engaged with their courses. Under most evaluation systems, such work is mostly invisible; however, the pandemic brought attention to the often unseen—and thus unevaluated and unrewarded—work done by dedicated teachers. As awareness of the many tasks involved in teaching increased, interest grew in developing more robust approaches to teaching evaluation that recognized and rewarded the full array of work instructors do. This approach advances a culture of greater appreciation and feelings of safety among faculty members—environmental factors that can help institutions retain faculty. Furthermore, since contingent and VITAL faculty handle many of the teaching responsibilities in their institutions, strengthening teaching evaluation helps bring more equity to the academy.[13]

Improving teaching evaluation also has institutional benefits beyond the experiences of the students and faculty. The approach to teaching evaluation described in this book, which encourages faculty to discuss the principles, values, and purposes informing their teaching and to incorporate multiple dimensions of teaching practice into evaluation processes, emphasizes institutional commitment to high-quality teaching. Highlighting commitment to excellence in educational practice and high-quality outcomes for students conveys important institutional values to the public. Thus, the approaches to teaching evaluation we discuss in this book make the value-propositions of high-quality teaching more transparent, an important consideration as institutions become more reliant on tuition and public perceptions of the quality of the outcomes they provide.

While reforming teaching evaluation can foster faculty discussion, encourage reflection, and heighten efforts to embrace effective teaching approaches, it can also create cultural challenges. Faculty prize their autonomy; observation by peers in a classroom is not customary and challenges the norm of that autonomy. Getting faculty buy-in or engagement in departmental efforts to change teaching evaluation is also difficult because of time constraints and pressures to prioritize research or other aspects of academic work over teaching. Teaching practice varies based on factors such as disciplinary culture, class size, type of class (laboratory, lecture, field work), level of course, and in-person or online context. These variations must be considered when developing new approaches to teaching evaluation. Additionally, departmental cultures, university leadership, and institutional priorities are relevant factors in shaping a change process around teaching evaluation. Thus, plans to reform teaching evaluation must recognize and honor the challenges inherent in the process and the diversity of contexts and approaches in which teaching occurs. But taking on this work has noteworthy benefits and outcomes. Efforts to engage in changing teaching evaluation, which is a form of organizational change, may contribute to more effective and rewarding teaching experiences, deeper student learning, and enhanced institutional reputation.

WHAT DOES THIS BOOK OFFER?

The framework for implementing high-quality teaching evaluation that we offer in this book focuses on seven dimensions of teaching that can provide a holistic assessment of the teaching contributions for all those instructing students. The book also explains how reforming teaching evaluation, particularly with the goal of providing more holistic assessments, requires systemic change, involving both individual departments and the whole institution. Institutional leaders working on new approaches to teaching evaluation can consider variations and adaptations of the strategies presented in this book. Those strategies were implemented in multiple departments at three universities and tailored to their unique contexts. We draw on those departmental examples (in different fields and disciplines) to illustrate practical steps, timelines, challenges, and choices departments face as they change their approach to teaching evaluation. Readers will gain understanding of effective, research-based approaches to teaching evaluation, as well as practical strategies for involving faculty and administrators in the process.

This approach to teaching evaluation provides a developmental roadmap for faculty seeking to improve their practices and provides a common language and structure that can span the institution while allowing for discipline-specific adaptations. The approach also addresses the proliferating concerns with commonly used methods of evaluating teaching, such as the well-documented age, gender, and race biases that can occur with student surveys. The system we are advancing counteracts such biases by drawing on multiple viewpoints and forms of evidence, allowing faculty to provide context and evidence about their teaching and elevate the work they do to help students learn. Our framework also provides a way to document, highlight, and examine the efforts a faculty member undertakes when engaged in substantive change in instructional approaches. An overreliance on end-of-term student surveys may penalize faculty for implementing novel, evidence-based teaching methods, which often result in an initial decrease of student survey scores, because they require more substantial cognitive engagment by students and conflict with students' expectations of a passive learning environment. The framework for teaching evaluation that we offer recognizes efforts to improve teaching methods and students' learning as good practice and points to additional sources of evidence (e.g., student learning outcomes, peer reviews) that can help contextualize student ratings.

This book draws on insights from a seven-year project, known as *TEval,* as it explores many facets of developing and using a new framework for evaluating teaching. This includes: (a) a rationale for transforming teaching evaluation; (b) a description of a research-based, developmental, and inclusive framework for approaching teaching evaluation; (c) examples and case studies showcasing different institutional approaches to implementing the framework; (d) guidance, analysis, and findings about systemic approaches to reforming teaching evaluation within different departmental and disciplinary contexts; (e) information on tools and practical processes to evaluate teaching; and (f) insights, findings, and lessons about institutional and departmental change processes to improve teaching evaluation.

WHAT RESEARCH SUPPORTS THE IDEAS IN THIS BOOK?

Since 2017, we have been carrying out an organizational change project called *TEval: A Study of Institutional Change to Advance STEM Undergraduate Education.* Our goal has been to advance the use of teaching evaluation approaches that are more equitable and holistic and that are aligned with what is known about effective and inclusive instructional practices. This work has been conducted with the support of a National Science Foundation grant and has involved three universities where the ideas have been incubated and tested: University of Colorado Boulder (CU), University of Kansas (KU), and University of Massachusetts Amherst (UMass). Four of the authors are each associated with one of these institutions and facilitated their institution's involvement in the project, and one of the authors has coordinated our research on the processes of change at these institutions.

The TEval project built on extensive prior work on representing and reviewing teaching with the goal of developing a framework, prototype materials, and institutional examples to enact evaluation approaches that are more transparent, developmental, and equitable.[14] In addition to focusing on development of the framework and related materials, the project also focused on developing and studying approaches to organizational change to embed these new approaches.

The framework (outlined in chapter 1) is organized around an adaptable, multidimensional rubric that externalizes expectations for teaching effectiveness, with seven dimensions to capture teaching in its totality (inside and out the classroom), along with guiding questions, defined expectations, and potential sources of evidence for each dimension.[15] To minimize bias and to make the fuller range of teaching contributions visible, it hinges on triangulating evidence from three lenses: instructor self-report (e.g., course materials, evidence of student learning and reflections on it); student voices (e.g., student surveys, alumni letters, focus groups); and a third-party/peer lens (e.g., class visits, review of course materials).[16] Information from these sources provides convergent evidence on effectiveness across the multiple dimensions of teaching activities and can be used for annual review, multiyear review for career progression decisions (such as promotion and tenure), and formative review and mentoring. A foundational feature of the approach is customization at the department or disciplinary level—where cultural factors play an important role in defining effective teaching—while also providing a level of uniformity across schools and colleges. The framework provides a starting point for departments and institutions to build consensus about what effective teaching looks like, a developmental roadmap for improving teaching practice, and a common structure and language for representing, reviewing and evaluating teaching.

Of course, the existence of a better framework does not guarantee that it will be enacted. The three universities and the departments within them that have been engaged in reforming teaching evaluation served as case studies through which we learned about the process of changing teaching evaluation, the usefulness of the framework, and the variations in approaches to using the framework as a vehicle for change. To support adaptation and use of the framework, the three universities collaborated as part of a project of the Bay View Alliance (BVA), supported by grant funding from the National Science Foundation. Together, they formed a networked improvement community to use the emerging framework to improve teaching evaluation and to learn together about the change process.[17] The campus work focused on department-level adoption of the framework. Departments are the main units for faculty evaluation at many institutions, and they are where faculty perceive themselves as having the most influence.[18] Informed by models of sensemaking and organizational learning, our change project involved guiding departments through a cycle of adapting, using, and refining the framework and associated tools and convening them regularly for reflection and knowledge exchange.[19] At all three universities, the enacting units have developed and tested models for other departments to adapt. Participants from each campus regularly shared experiences and results with colleagues from the other campuses at cross-campus knowledge exchanges.

We also engaged with university leadership to align with institutional priorities and processes and to pave the way for scaling up departmentally-based models. The department-level work has been accompanied by shifts in university-level processes around teaching evaluation. For example, at KU, multiple university-level processes (e.g., the annual review platform for teaching faculty and a revised student evaluation tool) have now been aligned with the TEval approach. At CU, TEval structures and processes have been embedded into college-level expectations for promotion and tenure in two colleges (arts and sciences and engineering). At UMass, principles encouraged by TEval were incorporated into revised union contracts for faculty.

Across the seven years of the project, we have collected data through interviews, observations, and document compilation and analysis, and engaged in comprehensive data analysis. Our goals have been to understand the various ways in which the framework can be used, the impact of use of the framework, the ways in which departments can engage in the process of changing teaching evaluation, and the role of leaders at the institution-level and the department-level in the change efforts. Comparative analysis has helped us to learn some generalizable principles about changing teaching evaluation.

The TEval project has made a great deal of progress in fostering better teaching evaluation processes and reward structures at the three implementation sites. Each campus has seen meaningful shifts in the ways in which teaching is documented and evaluated, moving toward a reward system that aligns with and encourages faculty use of effective, inclusive, and scholarly educational practices, and one that is more equitable and resistant to bias than traditional methods of evaluation. Across the three institutions, approximately eighty academic units (ranging from STEM fields to arts, humanities, social sciences, and business) have successfully integrated the TEval approach into evaluation processes (e.g., promotion and tenure, annual evaluation), often in combination with formative approaches (e.g., mentoring, peer review triads).

We have found the TEval framework and associated rubric to be a versatile tool in engaging colleagues and enacting change. It has empowered departments to move at their own pace in changing evaluation policies while providing considerable consistency across disciplines. The TEval project has also resulted in the development of related tools and resources to support more equitable and effective teaching evaluation systems. These include rubrics that externalize expectations for a broad range of teaching activities at varying levels of performance, protocols to guide peer review of teaching, guides for self-reflection, department templates for annual review, mapping tools to align evidence and artifacts with teaching dimensions, sample evaluation portfolios, supplements and glossaries on inclusive teaching elements, repositories of department adaptations and examples, and department-level case studies highlighting change processes. Additional resources include a website, www.TEval.net, where department guides, toolkits, and other useful artifacts are located.[20]

This work has also advanced our understanding of institutional change processes, particularly with respect to the high-stakes, fraught context of teaching evaluation. We have learned that the steps an institution takes to implement a change to teaching evaluation work optimally when aligned with the institution's culture around decision making. For example, if an institution's culture involves considerable faculty involvement and faculty voice in any decisions pertaining to teaching-related policies, then explicitly involving the appropriate faculty bodies in the process of making changes in teaching evaluation would be wise. At some institutions, that may mean involving college-level faculty advisory committees or, at the institution level, a faculty senate, other governance bodies, or a faculty union. The support of senior institutional leaders enhances departmental, college, and institutional efforts, and opportunities for faculty interaction to share processes and lessons contribute to successes across a university. The case studies of the three institutions have shown that change leaders must attend to barriers, engage faculty in sense-making as part of the change process, seek allies across the institution, and build toward sustainability and institutional embeddedness. Collaborations and partnerships are essential, both within and across institutions, to motivate participation, provide models and tools for practice, and foster adaptation to challenges that arise. We have also learned that while institutional contexts must be considered, common approaches and tools for teaching evaluation can be used across a wide array of institutions. Indeed, adaptations of the TEval framework and tools and other approaches to holistic teaching evaluation are beginning to be used at other institutions. Furthermore, national convenings about this work have demonstrated the increasing commitment across many universities and colleges to develop more robust and useful approaches to teaching evaluation and their interests in finding practical approaches, strategies, and tools for doing so.[21]

Overall, we have learned that taking a systemic approach to changing teaching evaluation that connects department-level, college-level, and central institutional efforts contributes to long-term success. The details of the department-level and institutional-level work, the examples of how to engage in systemic change to improve teaching evaluation, and the guidance that has emerged from our analyses for both institution-level and departmental leaders to engage in this kind of transformative work constitute the core content of this book.

WHAT INSTITUTIONAL STORIES WILL BE HIGHLIGHTED IN THIS BOOK?

Knowing a bit about the three institutions that we have studied and how they approached the process of changing teaching evaluation will help readers appreciate the examples we provide throughout the book and consider what contextual features may be similar to or different from their own institutional contexts. The stories of the three universities in our project, all guided by similar goals and a shared approach to effective teaching evaluation, show how plans to improve teaching evaluation may take different forms depending on the institutional context. The stories also illustrate the different roles that can be taken by provosts, deans, teaching center directors, and other institutional leaders, as the ground-level work unfolds within departments. Here, we provide short summaries of each university that participated in this project and highlight key elements of their approaches.

The University of Kansas

The KU effort sought to tap into growing faculty dissatisfaction with existing evaluation approaches and to widen faculty participation in course transformation around evidence-based practices. University policy requires that "multiple sources of information" be used for faculty evaluation, and it specifically identifies students, peers, and the faculty member as required sources in evaluation of progress toward tenure and promotion. Nonetheless, historically, the quality of the information collected and the way it was integrated and represented was highly variable. For instance, most peer evaluations consisted of an observation of a single class period followed by a letter describing the instructor's in-class performance. Instructor narratives typically centered on philosophy and what the instructor did, with little information about student learning and how it informs continued teaching practice. Review committees often lacked a shared vision of effective teaching and, faced with voluminous but information-poor materials, continued to gravitate toward the "clarity" provided by student ratings. In response to these challenges, the KU Center for Teaching Excellence (CTE) had developed a rubric to articulate a more complete view of effective teaching and scaffold teaching reviews that align with these ideals.

The team at KU that coordinated the TEval project consisted of the director and associate director of the CTE (both longtime faculty members), a faculty fellow at the center, and a program manager who was also based at the center. (The director and associate director of the center are two of the coauthors of this book.) The TEval project enabled the leaders to launch its Benchmarks for Teaching Effectiveness initiative, to advance department adaptation and use of the rubric and associated tools to transform teaching evaluation. The decision to situate the TEval work in the teaching center purposefully built on a significant history in which the CTE has earned considerable trust and respect across campus through its partnership with many departments on curricular and instructional projects. Drawing on the wide respect that CTE leaders receive and the positive experiences that a number of departments have had in CTE-facilitated projects, the KU center and its leaders invited departments to send teams to cross-departmental conversations about improving teaching evaluation. CTE also serves as an information hub for templates, examples, and tools, guides departmental teams, troubleshoots problems, and leads or participates in related institutional committees, such as to change promotion-and-tenure processes or student surveys of teaching. Participating departments in STEM, humanities, social sciences, and professional schools each worked through processes to decide on evidence that demonstrates effective teaching and ways to use the TEval framework to frame the evaluation processes in their units.

The TEval team also benefited from a partnership with the vice provost for faculty affairs, who embraced the project as it aligned with other institutional priorities around evaluation policies. The vice provost led campus-wide discussion on changes in the promotion and tenure guidelines and embedded the TEval rubric categories in an online system used for evaluating lecturers and teaching faculty. That online portal did not require departments to use the TEval approach but provided an option with drop-down menus that contained language from the rubric. The ease of that system drew many department chairs to use the TEval approach, at least for evaluating teaching professors, instructors, and adjunct faculty. The TEval effort also benefited from temporary policy changes brought on by the COVID-19 pandemic. When courses were forced into an emergency remote format in Spring 2020, faculty raised concerns about how disgruntled students would respond in student surveys of teaching. As a result, the university suspended use of student ratings in the evaluation system for three semesters. That left most departments with little sense of how to evaluate teaching, and the KU TEval team was able to offer its framework and rubric as a way forward. (How departments made progress is discussed in chapter 3.) The Center for Teaching Excellence played an important role in guiding, facilitating, and scaffolding the work of these departments. KU's successful early adopter cohorts included twenty-four departments and schools, and CTE continues to support academic units in adopting or refining TEval approaches.

The University of Colorado Boulder

When the TEval project began, CU had been working to transform undergraduate courses in STEM fields for two decades. Efforts through the Science Education Initiative, the Learning Assistant Program, and the Center for STEM Learning resulted in course transformations in fourteen departments in the College of Arts & Sciences and the College of Engineering and Applied Science. This work involved coordinated dialogues among faculty to define common goals and learning outcomes for courses within an academic unit, and the addition of support for course transformation with postdoctoral teaching fellows and embedded experts. Units ranging from engineering to German and Slavic languages engaged in the development and deployment of more robust, interactive, student-centered, and equitable practices in their courses along with associated assessments of student learning.[22] Although there had been substantial faculty engagement, sustaining the changes was sometimes difficult. Faculty engagement in such practices remains voluntary, and scholarly approaches to educational practices were not included in the evaluation process. The CU Office of Faculty Affairs requires that "dossiers for comprehensive review, tenure, or promotion must include multiple measures of teaching." However, the university lacked a well-defined framework to guide such measures, making it difficult to assess teaching quality or to encourage large numbers of faculty to improve their teaching. The TEval project created a framework that defines teaching as a scholarly activity (akin to research) and assesses core components of such scholarship.

This change effort has relied heavily on the enthusiasm, knowledge, and compelling engagement of a well-known physics faculty member (one of the coauthors of this book) who champions the power of effective teaching and articulates the goal of greater institutional commitment to improving teaching. He was also deeply involved with the Teaching Quality Framework (TQF) project, an earlier transformation initiative involving a number of departments. Emphasizing change at the department level, the CU approach to transformation of teaching evaluation has built on the well-established TQF project, in which a TQF central office works with institutional department action teams, which organize departmental committees facilitated and organized by institutional project leaders. The teams develop and share tools, practices, and processes across departments, encourage the change goals, and facilitate department-level change work. In the TEval work, a postdoctoral fellow has worked closely with departments to scaffold their work, provide materials adapted from the TEval rubric, and guide them through meetings to create forms and processes for departments to use for evaluation. Materials have been made available on a CU website. These department-based efforts have been supported by campus-wide discussions that have enabled common language, common approaches (student, peer, and faculty data sources), and campus-wide recognition for the adoption and use of these new measures. (See chapter 3.)

While faculty leadership has been the driving force at CU, early collaboration with key department chairs secured endorsement from the provost to address campus priorities around student success. After this early acknowledgment of the project, the subsequent support from deans has been critically important in scaling and sustaining the work to transform teaching evaluation. With the additional support of the deans of Arts and Sciences and the School of Business, the project scaled from STEM fields to a much broader representation of programs across campus. The faculty leader of the TEval project has purposely cultivated interest among several deans, who over time have committed to changing teaching evaluation and adopting the TEval approach within their colleges. Their advocacy, enthusiasm, and involvement as senior institutional leaders have been essential. Fueled by examples of various departmental successes, dean-level encouragement, and a strategically adept faculty leader, the change effort has found fertile ground in three colleges (Arts and Sciences, Business, and Engineering and Applied Science) and more than fifty departments. Standing support for this work now resides within the Center for Teaching and Learning.

The University of Massachusetts Amherst

The TEval efforts at UMass sought to build on university classroom initiatives and the efforts of a working group that aimed to expand the evaluation of teaching beyond student surveys. UMass made two high-profile investments in innovative teaching in the 2010s: the creation of two collaborative-learning classrooms and the construction of an integrated classroom building, which is home to a variety of innovative teaching spaces. Physical spaces where tables and other classroom equipment can be moved and reconfigured enable instructors to use a greater variety of teaching practices aligned with what is known about effective evidence-based teaching. For example, when an instructor can move classroom furniture from lecture style, in which chairs are lined up facing the teacher, to a group of tables that enable students to see each other and work together, more active learning, such as peer-to-peer interaction, is possible. The investment in new physical space at UMass was part of an effort by the administration to promote and encourage the use of evidence-based teaching practices. Faculty who are interested in teaching in these spaces must first complete training offered by the Institute for Teaching Excellence and Faculty Development (formerly the Center for Teaching) to learn about evidence-based teaching practices and best practices in course design. These investments were complemented by a new section of the campus strategic plan focused on student success and teaching. However, there was a disconnect between the administration's goal of increasing student success through better teaching and the way teaching was evaluated.

For many years, UMass has based teaching evaluation on student surveys using a set of questions each with five-point response choices. The correlation of such instruments to objective measures of teaching effectiveness has never been demonstrated. The disconnect between the use of such surveys and effective teaching became apparent, in part, because of the new collaborative learning classrooms themselves. Faculty response to the spaces was positive, but an analysis of student ratings showed a decrease in scores for faculty who changed the pedagogy of their courses to better suit these new spaces, usually with a rebound after a year or two. It became clear by 2015 that a more effective method of teaching evaluation was needed.

An associate dean for student success analytics, who is also a chemistry professor (and one of the coauthors of this book), and a postdoctoral fellow were the key facilitators for work on teaching evaluation at UMass. Their leadership built on the efforts of a working group created in 2016 to develop recommendations for improving teaching evaluation. The working group reviewed research and policy literature, considered practices at the UMass campus, and discussed new approaches to teaching evaluation as a way to better promote evidence-based teaching practices. Project leaders also engaged leaders of the faculty union for their support, as the union had to approve any changes in the evaluation system. The TEval team promoted the TEval rubric at UMass as a way to address the disconnect between teaching and evaluation, and as a way to adopt an evaluation system that did not rely solely on student surveys. The TEval approach also aligned with the UMass faculty collective bargaining unit's emphasis on holistic teaching evaluation. Goals included consistency across different approaches to teaching and different disciplines, and better alignment with known approaches to effective teaching. The approach also had to be feasible for departments and faculty to incorporate, and practical for administrators to use in making promotion and merit determinations.

Nine departments from across four colleges at UMass have been involved in the project. An initial pilot cohort of departments met every few weeks to discuss their approaches to changing teaching evaluation, but most departments have worked independently as their time allows, with the option to call on the TEval project leader for advice. Periodic meetings of departmental leaders, convened by the TEval project leader, to share experiences with designing and implementing more holistic evaluation approaches have supported the work, as have departmental visits and consultations with the TEval project leaders. Influenced by this work, the annual faculty report template for the university now includes elements of the TEval rubric.

Overall Comments About the Institutional Cases

The leaders of the TEval work at Colorado, Kansas, and UMass had similar goals to change teaching evaluation. Yet, each has been sensitive and responsive to their specific institutional contexts. The cases illustrate different approaches to institutional change that advance more robust and productive approaches to teaching evaluation. Each institution's culture and history have influenced which approaches have been most feasible for advancing change. These institutional cases will be used as examples throughout the book. We urge readers to use these examples as background as they consider how the ideas in this book can be adapted to their own institutional contexts.

WHO IS THIS BOOK WRITTEN FOR AND HOW IS IT ORGANIZED?

This book is addressed to administrative and faculty leaders interested in changing teaching evaluation at the departmental, college, and campus levels. We also hope those who study change in higher education will find the framework, examples, and analyses of processes to transform teaching evaluation helpful in examining how significant change occurs in higher education. For both audiences, we have aimed for a style that is accessible, straightforward, and engaging while also meeting the expectations of those in higher education for evidence-based claims. Readers will find explanations informed by research, rationale and conceptualizations, and practical strategies that can motivate and guide professional practice. The book presents the transformation of teaching evaluation as a form of systemic organizational change, and provides practical guidelines for leaders interested in effective campus-based, systemic transformation of teaching evaluation. We put particular emphasis on the importance of considering variations and particularities in departmental and institutional cultures.

The rest of this book is organized in five chapters:

- Chapter 1 provides an overview of the TEval framework for evaluating teaching. The chapter explains the dimensions of the TEval rubric for evaluating teaching and ways departments and institutions can use it to define and evaluate teaching effectiveness. Chapter 1 provides both the rationale underlying the rubric and practical guidance for using it.
- Chapter 2 discusses the research and theory about organizational change in higher education that inform and explain the practical suggestions provided in the book. It provides the background for those who want to understand the "why" of using various strategies and approaches to transform teaching evaluation.
- Chapter 3 focuses on departments, which are the central location for most efforts to transform teaching evaluation—not surprisingly, since faculty members typically engage in their work as teachers within the context of their home departments. Chapter 3 explains different approaches departments can take to change teaching evaluation and provides a number of examples from the departments we have studied. Department chairs will find practical guidance in this chapter.

- In chapter 4, we recognize efforts to transform teaching evaluation as a form of institutional change in which leadership, professional development, alignment with institutional priorities, and monitoring and feedback efforts are important levers for change. Informed by the theory and research discussed in chapter 2, we specifically address senior-level institutional leaders, especially provosts, deans, and teaching center directors, and provide them with clear and practical advice relevant to their key roles in the change process.
- Finally, in chapter 5, we step back and situate the discussion of transformative, systemic change of teaching evaluation in the national context. In the last few years, we have seen many higher education institutions turning attention to teaching evaluation, especially as they seek to enhance the quality of teaching at their institutions. With this growing interest, institutions are looking for ways to create alliances and collaborations to work together and share emerging lessons as they experiment with approaches to reform teaching evaluation. Institutional leaders are recognizing the critical importance of their teaching mission and are seeking effective approaches to improve teaching. More robust, inclusive, and equitable approaches to teaching evaluation constitute important levers for elevating teaching, highlighting institutional commitment to continuous improvement, and providing faculty with recognition and support in their own efforts to enhance their teaching in service to deeper student learning.

HOW SHOULD READERS USE THE BOOK?

We recognize that readers will have different reasons for using this book. Some will want to move through it in the order the chapters are presented. Others may want to take a more targeted, tactical approach. For example, those leading departments or chairing faculty committees may want to read chapter 1 to understand the TEval Framework and then jump to either chapter 3, with its focus on department leaders, or chapter 4, with its attention to how institutional leaders can support efforts to transform teaching evaluation. Those readers interested in theory and research will appreciate the "deep dive" on these topics in chapter 2. Senior institutional leaders will find the combination of chapters 1 and 4 particularly informative for broad institutional application of the holistic approach to teaching evaluation. Policy makers may choose to use chapter 5 as guidance for their own reflections, conversations, and cross-institutional efforts pertaining to the transformation of teaching evaluation as a lever in broader agendas to strengthen the quality of teaching and learning for a diverse population of learners. Case studies, examples, and related resources that supplement this book can be found on the TEval website at www.TEval.net.

We see a revised evaluation process as an opportunity to reinvigorate the teaching community and to elevate the importance of teaching and learning in higher education. Reform in teaching evaluation is also a strong tool for strengthening undergraduate education. Arguably, colleges and universities have grown comfortable and complacent with a deeply flawed system of evaluating teaching—a system that has obscured the complexities involved in effective teaching. The TEval approach discussed in this book can help universities find a meaningful path to strengthening the quality of the teaching mission. It helps them articulate the value of teaching and set clearer, more meaningful standards for faculty. It also helps reward faculty for the substantial time and intellectual work that goes into teaching. The approach discussed in this book also promotes accountability for instruction and provides avenues for faculty to receive meaningful feedback on teaching. Universities and colleges that transform their approach to teaching evaluation are engaged in the broader institutional and cultural change needed to deepen student learning, respond to the increasing public dissatisfaction in higher education, and ensure all the instructional staff can do their work in an environment that recognizes and values the full array of work involved in effective teaching, including continuous improvement of teaching and learning.

1

The TEval Approach to Transforming the Evaluation of Teaching

THE TEVAL APPROACH TO transforming teaching evaluation centers on a common scholarly framework and a corresponding rubric. In addition to supporting holistic teaching evaluation, the framework is designed to foster collaborative examination of multiple aspects of teaching among faculty in a department or academic unit. Unlike end-of-term student surveys of teaching, which center on performance in individual courses, the TEval approach is designed to evaluate the instructor's overall body of work in teaching.

The TEval approach guided the work of departments across the three case universities (University of Kansas, University of Colorado Boulder, and University of Massachusetts Amherst), whose efforts provide the data and examples supporting the ideas for practice offered in this book. This chapter steps through the dimensions of the TEval framework and rubric, describing the underlying rationale for these tools as well as the practical guidance for using them, which will be explored further in later chapters. We provide an overview of the TEval approach here not only as a means to adopting or adapting similar approaches in your own institution but also as a means to understand the context for the discussions in the following chapters.

A COMMON FRAMEWORK

The TEval approach draws on twenty-five years of work on scholarly teaching and its evaluation and related work on the peer review of teaching.[1] The framework guiding the TEval approach provides a richer, more complete view of teaching practice and the evidence that speaks to it than most commonly used measures.[2]

The framework specifies that multiple dimensions of teaching activities should be evaluated to capture the teaching endeavor in its totality, including aspects that take place outside the learning space (whether that be a classroom, a lab, the field, or an online space) and that go beyond the teaching of individual courses. Together, these dimensions provide a comprehensive definition of high-quality educational practice. While we have specified a set of seven dimensions in our own work, alternative configurations are possible, and departments, programs, or institutions can customize the dimensions to suit their needs, as we will explore in subsequent chapters. These dimensions not only help guide the evaluation process but they also articulate the values of the organization and of the individuals within it with respect to educating students. Notably, many academic units have never explicitly discussed or codified their shared values regarding students learning. Even engaging in this step alone can be valuable.

Components of the Framework: How They Function and Why They Are Important

Dimensions

The TEval framework specifies seven dimensions of teaching for evaluation:

1) Goals, content, and alignment
2) Teaching practices used

3) Class climate
4) Achievement of learning goals
5) Reflection and iterative growth
6) Mentoring and advising
7) Involvement in teaching service, scholarship, or community

Effective use of the framework involves evaluating each dimension with more than one form of evidence and through more than one "lens." A lens is a viewpoint offered by a particular individual, such as the students, instructor, or a third party external to the course.

The framework includes guiding questions for each dimension and descriptions of teaching practices or criteria categorized into three quality tiers (such as "developing," "proficient," and "accomplished"). These descriptions of performance provide scaffolding and feedback to improve teaching while also structuring the evaluation process.

Guiding Questions for Each Dimension of the Framework

Dimension 1: Goals, Content, and Alignment

What are students expected to learn from the courses taught? Are learning goals clearly articulated in a way that is accessible to all students? Are course goals appropriate for the course as part of the larger curriculum and for the audience for which it is intended? Are topics appropriately challenging and related to current issues in the field? Are the materials high-quality and aligned with course goals? Does the content represent diverse perspectives? Are assessments aligned with course goals?

Dimension 2: Teaching Practices

How is in-class and out-of-class time used? Are assignments, assessments, and learning activities designed to help all students learn?

What effective or high-impact methods are used to improve understanding and engage all students in learning? Do in- and out-of-class activities provide opportunities for practice and feedback on important skills and concepts? Are forms of assessment varied to allow for the success of diverse learners?

Dimension 3: Class Climate

To what extent is the class climate respectful, supportive, and cooperative? Does it encourage motivation and engagement for all students? Do all students feel included? How are student-student and student-instructor dialogue fostered? What are the students' views of their learning experiences? How has the instructor sought student feedback, and how has feedback informed the instructor's teaching?

Dimension 4: Achievement of Learning Outcomes

Does the instructor clearly communicate the learning goals for the course? What evidence is used to determine the degree to which students achieve the defined course goals? How well are course assignments, assessments, and learning activities aligned with the defined learning goals? Are there efforts to ensure that all students have equitable opportunities to achieve the learning goals? Are standards for evaluating learning clear and connected to program, curriculum, or professional expectations? Does the quality of learning support success in other contexts?

Dimension 5: Reflection and Iterative Growth

How and why has the instructor's teaching changed over time? How have changes been informed by evidence of student learning and student feedback? How has peer feedback been incorporated as changes in the instructor's teaching over time? How have the instructor's goals for their courses and students changed over time?

Dimension 6: Mentoring and Advising

How effectively has the instructor worked individually with undergraduate or graduate students? Does the instructor establish clear, individualized and responsive expectations for student and mentor? Does the instructor provide constructive and timely coaching and feedback? How does the quality of and time commitment to mentoring fit with disciplinary and departmental expectations?

Dimension 7: Involvement in Teaching Service, Scholarship, or Community

How has the instructor contributed to the broader teaching community, both on and off campus? Areas of contribution can include the learning culture in the department or institution (e.g., curriculum committees, program assessment, cocurricular activities); engaging with peers on or off campus in teaching communities, workshops, peer reviews, or similar activities; educational leadership activities (e.g., leading teaching workshops, presentations or publications about teaching, grants related to teaching).

Multiple Lenses and Forms of Evidence

The framework also specifies that multiple lenses (sources of data) should be used to evaluate each dimension of teaching. The lenses, or voices, include the instructor being evaluated, students in courses taught by that instructor, and a third party. The third party may be another instructor in the department or a person external to the department who has specialized knowledge of the subject matter or of pedagogy (such as a staff member of a teaching and learning center). For some aspects of the teaching work, such as teaching-related publications or community activities, the third party may be external to the institution. Indeed, several people may contribute to the evidence collected as fits the needs of each dimension and each instructor's activities. Overall, the goal is

FIGURE 1.1 Different lenses can provide input for different dimensions

	Student lens	Instructor lens	Third party lens
Dimension 1	✓	✓	
Dimension 2		✓	✓
Dimension 3	✓	✓	✓
...	✓		✓

to have more than one voice speaking to each dimension, as exemplified in figure 1.1. Doing so will provide greater validity to the analysis by expanding the perspectives on an instructor's work rather than overrelying on any given lens.

In a similar vein to using multiple lenses, the TEval approach recommends using multiple forms of evidence. This will mostly take care of itself when ensuring that there are at least two voices for each dimension. The goal of using multiple forms of evidence is, again, to increase the validity of the analysis by compensating for the inherent biases and limitations of any single type of measure. Information from these sources should be triangulated to provide convergent evidence on multiple categories of teaching activities.

The following are examples of evidence that can be gathered to represent different voices for each dimension.

Multiple Lenses and Forms of Evidence for Evaluating Each Dimension

Dimension 1: Goals, Content, and Alignment

Instructor: Syllabus (course goals), sample materials (rubrics, assignment sheets, readings), instructor narrative.

Student: Student survey of teaching, instructor-gathered feedback.

Third Party: Peer review, program or curriculum map, feedback on quality of materials.

Dimension 2: Teaching Practices

Instructor: Syllabus/schedule, sample class activities, assignments and lesson plans, example feedback on student work, instructor narrative.

Student: Student survey of teaching, instructor-gathered feedback.

Third Party: Class observation guided by an observation tool or protocol to categorize activities in a class. Review of course materials, including the design of exams and assignments and their alignment with communicated learning goals.

Dimension 3: Class Climate

Instructor: Syllabus, sample class activities and lesson plans, instructor narrative, reflections on student feedback.

Student: Student survey of teaching, instructor-gathered feedback.

Third Party: Class observation, focus group discussion with students.

Dimension 4: Achievement of Learning Goals

Instructor: Sample assessments and rubrics, student work samples, summary or analysis of student performance, instructor narrative.

Student: Student survey of teaching, instructor-gathered feedback, student reflection or self-assessment of learning.

Third Party: Review of course materials and student work.

Dimension 5: Reflection and Iterative Growth

Instructor: Syllabi and course materials highlighting changes in the course, evidence of changes in student achievement, instructor narrative.

Student: Changes in student feedback.

Third Party: Review of course materials, observation of the class.

Dimension 6: Mentoring and Advising

Instructor: Instructor statement, CV (e.g., number of student mentees and status, service on student committees, letters of recommendation or nomination of students for awards, scholarship with student collaborators).

Student: Letters or surveys from student advisees.

Third Party: If possible, conversations with student advisees.

Dimension 7: Involvement in Teaching Service, Scholarship, or Community

Instructor: CV (e.g., internal or external workshops, presentations, articles, media, grants; participation in communities or development opportunities), teaching committees, involvement in experiential learning or cocurricular activities.

Public Artifacts: Publications or other public repositories of teaching practices or results, announcements of presentations or workshops.

Third Party: Feedback about public events or outreach efforts.

When using the TEval holistic framework for teaching evaluation, departments can determine which dimensions are most relevant and what forms of evidence they will gather for each dimension. Whether that choice is left up to the instructor being evaluated or is made in a departmental process or committee is up to each department. A later chapter will describe different departmental approaches for determining the dimensions and forms of evidence to be used.

Performance Criteria

The TEval framework uses a rubric to articulate the criteria for determining the level of performance of the instructor being evaluated. The terminology used to describe each level can have a substantive impact on the ways that instructors interpret them and the ways that evaluators use them. We propose three levels of performance. In this way, a discussion among faculty in a department can focus initially on determining the qualities and criteria of the middle level. The level above, then, represents activities or achievements that surpass expectations, and the level below represents those that are still approaching the goal. If a department were to use four or five levels, it would need to make increasingly narrow distinctions among levels of achievement. Those distinctions can be difficult to articulate and challenging for department members to agree on.

The middle level is where we would expect most instructors to fall on many dimensions. Because the evaluation process should provide a means for continuous improvement, the first level is what would be expected of instructors who are still honing their skills. On the other end of the scale, the top level should not be one that most instructors would reach very quickly. Because the framework centers continuous improvement and responsiveness as fundamental to effective teaching, even at the top level instructors are expected to remain attentive and responsive to student learning and committed to ongoing enhancement. Overall, the absence of improvement efforts over time across multiple dimensions constitutes poor performance.

Following are examples of the nomenclature used for the performance levels at each of our three institutions. Some evolved over time or changed within an institution after initial trials. The best set of labels at your institution will depend on the institutional culture and history. For example, one of the TEval institutions has used the labels "developing," "proficient," and "expert," whereas another has used "entry into teaching/requires improvement," "basic skill/competent," and "professional/advanced."

The rubric also provides specific criteria for each level of each dimension (figure 1.2 provides an example of criteria used at the University of Kansas). Complete rubrics are available on the companion website to this book (www.TEval.net) and can be used as is, without adaptation.

FIGURE 1.2 Detailed criteria for each dimension in the rubric from the University of Kansas

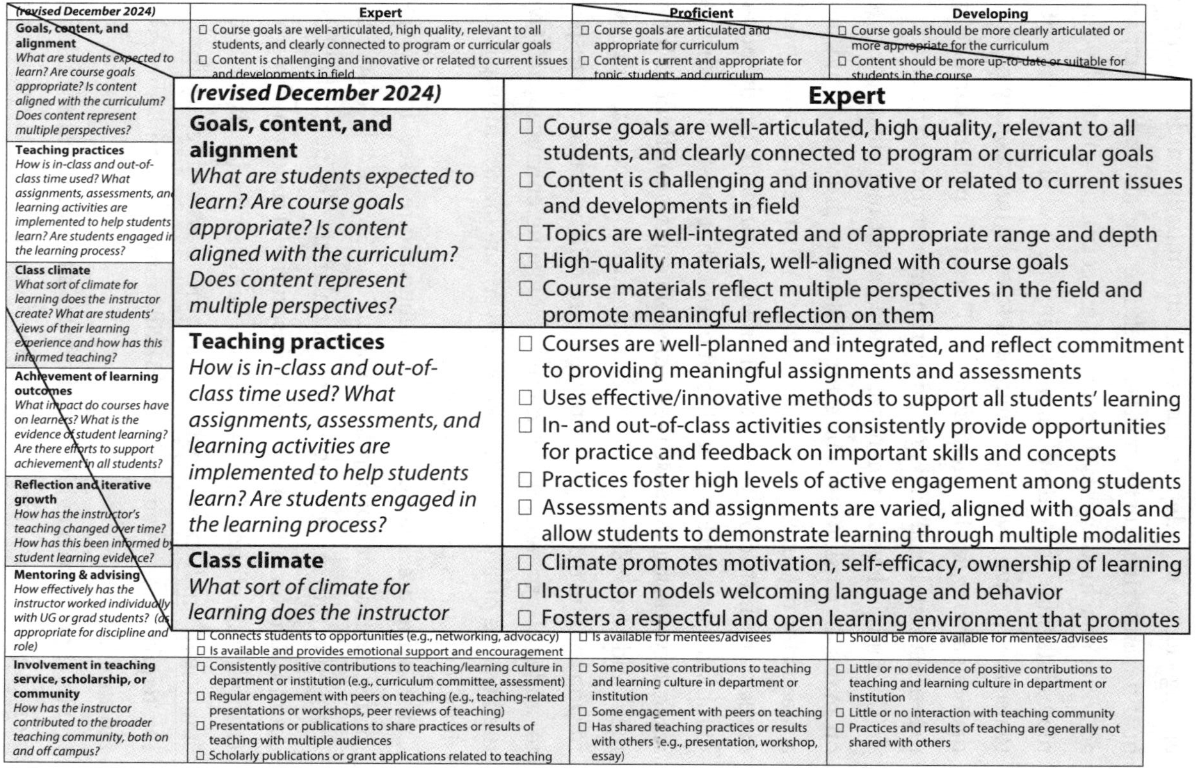

(revised December 2024)	Expert	Proficient	Developing
Goals, content, and alignment *What are students expected to learn? Are course goals appropriate? Is content aligned with the curriculum? Does content represent multiple perspectives?*	☐ Course goals are well-articulated, high quality, relevant to all students, and clearly connected to program or curricular goals ☐ Content is challenging and innovative or related to current issues and developments in field	☐ Course goals are articulated and appropriate for curriculum ☐ Content is current and appropriate for topic, students, and curriculum	☐ Course goals should be more clearly articulated or more appropriate for the curriculum ☐ Content should be more up-to-date or suitable for students in the course
Teaching practices *How is in-class and out-of-class time used? What assignments, assessments, and learning activities are implemented to help students learn? Are students engaged in the learning process?*			
Class climate *What sort of climate for learning does the instructor create? What are students' views of their learning experience and how has this informed teaching?*			
Achievement of learning outcomes *What impact do courses have on learners? What is the evidence of student learning? Are there efforts to support achievement in all students?*			
Reflection and iterative growth *How has the instructor's teaching changed over time? How has this been informed by student learning evidence?*			
Mentoring & advising *How effectively has the instructor worked individually with UG or grad students? (as appropriate for discipline and role)*	☐ Connects students to opportunities (e.g., networking, advocacy) ☐ Is available and provides emotional support and encouragement	☐ Is available for mentees/advisees	☐ Should be more available for mentees/advisees
Involvement in teaching service, scholarship, or community *How has the instructor contributed to the broader teaching community, both on and off campus?*	☐ Consistently positive contributions to teaching/learning culture in department or institution (e.g., curriculum committee, assessment) ☐ Regular engagement with peers on teaching (e.g., teaching-related presentations or workshops, peer reviews of teaching) ☐ Presentations or publications to share practices or results of teaching with multiple audiences ☐ Scholarly publications or grant applications related to teaching	☐ Some positive contributions to teaching and learning culture in department or institution ☐ Some engagement with peers on teaching ☐ Has shared teaching practices or results with others (e.g., presentation, workshop, essay)	☐ Little or no evidence of positive contributions to teaching and learning culture in department or institution ☐ Little or no interaction with teaching community ☐ Practices and results of teaching are generally not shared with others

(revised December 2024)	Expert
Goals, content, and alignment *What are students expected to learn? Are course goals appropriate? Is content aligned with the curriculum? Does content represent multiple perspectives?*	☐ Course goals are well-articulated, high quality, relevant to all students, and clearly connected to program or curricular goals ☐ Content is challenging and innovative or related to current issues and developments in field ☐ Topics are well-integrated and of appropriate range and depth ☐ High-quality materials, well-aligned with course goals ☐ Course materials reflect multiple perspectives in the field and promote meaningful reflection on them
Teaching practices *How is in-class and out-of-class time used? What assignments, assessments, and learning activities are implemented to help students learn? Are students engaged in the learning process?*	☐ Courses are well-planned and integrated, and reflect commitment to providing meaningful assignments and assessments ☐ Uses effective/innovative methods to support all students' learning ☐ In- and out-of-class activities consistently provide opportunities for practice and feedback on important skills and concepts ☐ Practices foster high levels of active engagement among students ☐ Assessments and assignments are varied, aligned with goals and allow students to demonstrate learning through multiple modalities
Class climate *What sort of climate for learning does the instructor*	☐ Climate promotes motivation, self-efficacy, ownership of learning ☐ Instructor models welcoming language and behavior ☐ Fosters a respectful and open learning environment that promotes

An alternative approach, implemented at one of our institutions, is to engage the members of the department or program unit in defining only the "proficient" level (or equivalent) for each dimension. That will then be the benchmark for determining whether an instructor is at, above, or below "proficient" or its equivalent. This type of conversation among the members of the department is a continuation of the collaborative sensemaking around the teaching mission of the group and provides a powerful foundation from which to build a shared understanding of the teaching goals of the academic unit. To use the rubric for personnel evaluations, departments will need to map these performance levels onto their annual evaluation criteria. For example, at an institution with a 1 (poor) to 5 (excellent) evaluation scale for promotion and tenure, a department could specify that instructors who consistently perform in the top tier across dimensions receive an "excellent" rating, those with a mix of top and middle receive a "very good" rating, and so on. Departments could also consider setting expectations that vary for instructors in different career phases (e.g., setting a higher bar for an excellent rating for senior faculty than for early career faculty). Again, complete rubrics are available on the companion website to this book (www.TEval.net).

Cross-Cutting Elements

In addition to the specific dimensions, several cross-cutting themes run across the dimensions. These themes are based on current understanding of best practices for effective teaching and, thus, reflected in the criteria used. The first of these is inclusive and equitable practice. As has been highlighted in reports and research literature, teaching can only be considered excellent if it uses equitable practices that create a sense of belonging among students and an environment that empowers them to learn.[3] An example of this cross-cutting theme can be seen in the dimension titled "Goals, Content, and Alignment," which includes a consideration of the materials or examples reflecting diverse perspectives and backgrounds. Similarly, the "Teaching Practices" dimension evaluates the methods employed to support all students' learning and the use of varied forms of assessment. "Class Climate" considers whether welcoming language is used and the ways that students are encouraged to participate and learn. This theme, then, is part of all the dimensions and of the overall consideration of the quality of teaching being evaluated.

A second cross-cutting theme is the centering of student learning. The centering of student learning shapes the ways a course is designed—starting with deep consideration of what students need to know and why and culminating with the selection of methods for students to demonstrate their learning. The "Teaching Practices" dimension emphasizes course implementation of practices that are also tuned to student learning through learning activities that actively engage students' reasoning and provide opportunities for practice and feedback on key skills and concepts. In the dimension "Reflection and Iterative Growth," consideration of student learning outcomes is a primary compass guiding an instructor's pedagogical refinements.

Additional cross-cutting themes may emerge within a given department or institution. For instance, a fine arts program might prioritize student practice and performance as a fundamental component across all courses. Similarly, institutional leaders may define campus-wide commitments to be reflected across all academic units. For example, institutions where experiential learning is a key priority may expect integration of experiential learning throughout various disciplinary programs.

Using Different Forms of Evidence

Building a comprehensive understanding of an instructor's teaching performance requires collecting and analyzing a variety of evidence from multiple sources. However, consulting with numerous departments has shown us that attempting to consider and collect evidence related to all aspects of the TEval framework simultaneously can seem overwhelming. Instead, it is helpful to consider which pieces of this process are already part of the evaluation system being used in a given department or institution. After beginning with these, a department can add other aspects in a stepwise manner as it becomes familiar with the approach. All forms of evidence have limitations. Using multiple forms of evidence as part of the review, though, smooths the "noise" caused by biases inherent in any *single* information source. As will be discussed in later chapters, achieving sustainable changes and developing a mindset of continuous improvement in teaching depends on having forms of measurement that faculty and administrators trust. The TEval approach emphasizes that no single piece of evidence should stand alone; rather, the synthesis of multiple forms creates a richer, more valid assessment.

Collecting an array of evidence can be done by different individuals or coordinated by a single individual in preparation for review. For example, if a department or program has a person or subcommittee that reviews materials for promotion evaluations, this person or committee may want to be in control of requesting the various forms of data they want to see for each dimension. Alternatively, a department may request that the instructor being evaluated compile some portions of the needed data and provide it in a review-ready format or through an online portal.

Each of the sections below addresses both the tools for evaluation and the processes by which they are implemented as a component of holistic teaching evaluation, with the understanding that these will need to be locally defined and adapted. The sources of evidence and data collection protocols referenced in the framework are available through our repositories on www.TEval.net. Some of these tools, along with their associated protocols for data collection and evaluation, can be adopted by departments as-is, while others may require adaptation to fit specific local contexts.

Instructor Narrative and Reflection

An instructor's self-reflective narrative about their teaching is a valuable form of evidence that highlights the intellectual work involved in effective teaching and the improvement of student learning. An informative narrative does more than share a teaching philosophy—it describes what an instructor teaches, how they teach it, why they chose those particular approaches, and what evidence shows those methods work. Just as importantly, a strong narrative also addresses how the instructor has evolved in their teaching practices over time, including responding to student feedback, shifts in course content to stay current, or new strategies implemented to improve student learning. The instructor's willingness to critically examine their own teaching and make informed adjustments demonstrates their commitment to professional development and their scholarly approach to teaching. The instructor narrative will also provide context for materials provided by students and third-party reviewers as part of the overall evaluation.

Course Syllabi

Course syllabi will usually need to originate from the instructor unless departments regularly maintain a repository. A review committee can evaluate the syllabus by looking for specific elements, including whether the course goals are clearly articulated, appropriately challenging, and relevant to the field of study. Additionally, syllabi should demonstrate inclusivity through the language used, indication of students' access to the instructor, and incorporation of diverse perspectives about the content and equitable learning opportunities. The syllabus can provide insight into the instructor's intentional planning and course design. Course syllabi can become even more informative if combined with an instructor narrative describing course design, goals, and assessments. This instructor narrative can be a written document, or it may originate as part of the conversation that guides the third-party observation process (see below).

Course Materials

Course materials, including assignments, rubrics, and readings, offer another layer of evidence about the quality of teaching. They reflect the instructor's ability to select and structure content and instructional activities that align with learning objectives and address diverse learner needs. High-quality materials should encourage critical thinking, engagement, and application of knowledge. Evaluators should assess whether the materials support active learning, provide opportunities for practice and feedback, and are accessible to all students. Additionally, evaluators can examine how course materials evolve over time, showing evidence of reflection and iterative growth in response to student performance and feedback. As is the case with syllabi, course materials are more informative and easier to review if combined with an instructor narrative that provides evaluators a guide to the materials. In this way, course materials serve as supporting documentation for statements made in the instructor's self-reflective narrative.

Course Portfolio

A course portfolio—a carefully curated collection of materials unified by a course narrative—is a particularly robust and cohesive way for an instructor to demonstrate both the practical and intellectual aspects of their teaching through the lens of a specific course. The course narrative serves as the backbone of the portfolio; it explains the course objectives, the pedagogical methods chosen to help students achieve the objectives, the rationale for those choices, and how the instructor evaluates whether these methods are working. Through the narrative, instructors can tell the story of their course—from its foundational goals to its practical implementation and outcomes for student learning. The portfolio also includes supporting documentation that, along with the course narrative, paints a comprehensive picture of the course: a detailed syllabus that outlines the course structure and objectives, a representative assignment with assessment criteria, a sample learning activity, and evidence or examples of student learning. Each element should be chosen to align with and support the core course objectives established in the narrative, creating a cohesive demonstration of teaching excellence.

Representations (or Evidence) of Student Learning

The TEval framework centers student learning. Direct evidence of the impact of teaching on student learning outcomes can be provided through samples of student work, such as graded assignments, projects, exams, and more comprehensive summaries of student performance on assessments and assignments. Samples of student work provide evaluators with concrete illustrations of the quality of student awareness and achievement of course objectives and how stated course goals are driving the materials and activities of the course. Moreover, student work can highlight whether assessment strategies are inclusive and equitable, offering all students a fair opportunity to demonstrate their understanding. Summaries of patterns in student performance provide a broader description of the levels of learning exhibited in the class as a whole. For instance, information about the distributions of performance on different components of an assessment or on different dimensions of a rubric can reveal areas where the course is supporting robust learning and where adjustments may be needed. Ideally, longitudinal evidence of student learning can be reviewed to assess changes in the quality of materials or student performance over time.

Student Perspectives: Surveys, Letters, or Focus Group Summaries

As discussed above, the student perspective is a relevant component of the holistic approach. Student perspectives captured through an end-of-term instrument can provide a snapshot of student views about a course; these can be affected by the proximity to the experience ("can't see the forest for the trees") and the general stressfulness of end-of-term activities. Student feedback, then, is often more useful when gathered after students have had an opportunity to see the effects of their learning in later classes or in internships, jobs, or other activities. Collected through letters, surveys, or focus group discussions, these student perspectives can add an invaluable dimension to the evaluation process. These narratives provide insight into the students' lived experiences with respect to the course, both in terms of the content learned and the instructor's ability to create an inclusive and supportive learning environment. Focus groups can be used after a course has ended with students who are still at the institution (if the focus of the evaluation is a course taught earlier in the curriculum, for example). A different form of focus group, sometimes referred to as a classroom interview, can be carried out with students in the course, possibly by the person doing class observations. Finally, letters or survey responses can be solicited from graduates. With the widespread availability of online communication tools, it is also possible to arrange for focus groups of students who are no longer at the institution.

In-Class Observations

Classroom observations offer a real-time perspective on the instructor's teaching practices. Whether conducted by peers, external reviewers, or trained observers, classroom observations can assess classroom dynamics, the use of instructional strategies, and the overall learning climate. Observers should focus on how the instructor facilitates student engagement, encourages collaboration, and adapts to the needs of diverse learners. To provide some structure and context for observation by a peer instructor, it is strongly recommended that the observer and instructor meet in advance of any classroom observations to discuss the course goals, teaching strategies, and what both parties would like to learn from the observation (see next paragraph). Peer review protocols and rubrics, including those developed by the TEval project, can provide additional structure and consistency to peer observations. Structured observation tools, such as the COPUS (Classroom Observation Protocol for Undergraduate STEM), the RTOP (Reformed Teaching Observation Protocol), or the PAITE (Protocol for Advancing Inclusive Teaching Efforts), implemented by trained observers, are another approach for ensuring consistency and rigor in class observations.[4] However, it is important to recognize that a single observation will have limited usefulness. The dynamic of a class often changes daily and evolves over a semester. Also, a classroom observer is likely to disrupt the class routine, affecting both students and the instructor.

Peer-to-Peer Dialogue and Review

A structured dialogue between an instructor and peer reviewer, organized around a set of materials, can uncover the complex intellectual work that underlies effective and inclusive teaching and provide important context for what is visible in a classroom observation. By examining course materials, learning objectives, assessment strategies, and student work samples together, this sort of peer review process enables instructors to articulate their pedagogical reasoning, explaining why they made specific course design choices, how they respond to student learning needs, and how they adapt their teaching to evolving departmental and disciplinary standards. Thus, the peer reviewer (who may also observe one or more class periods) gains insight into how the instructor prepares for a course, develops syllabi, establishes learning objectives, selects materials, designs activities and assessments, provides feedback to learners, and manages classroom dynamics, and how these choices are related to student performance. This approach treats teaching as scholarly work worthy of serious intellectual discussion, creating opportunities for constructive feedback on design and implementation. Often, the dialogue becomes developmental for both parties, helping both the instructor and the reviewer reflect on pedagogical teaching choices and how well they are working. Another advantage of this type of peer review process is that it is appropriate for all course modalities, including traditional in-person courses and asynchronous online courses.

Summary of Teaching-Related Outreach Activities

Instructors often engage in teaching-related activities that extend beyond the classroom. Outreach activities, such as contributing to curriculum improvements, participating in professional development, conducting a peer review, or facilitating workshops, are important indicators of the instructor's broader impact on the teaching community. A summary of these activities demonstrates the instructor's commitment to continuous improvement and their role in enhancing educational practices within and beyond their institution.

Published Articles

Finally, publications and presentations related to teaching, such as journal articles, conference proceedings, book chapters, podcasts, and other creative work in nonacademic outlets, provide an additional lens through which to evaluate an instructor's contributions to the field. These articles often represent the culmination of reflective practice, research, and innovation in teaching. By sharing their work publicly, instructors contribute to the broader discourse on education, highlighting their expertise and commitment to advancing teaching scholarship.

BUILT FOR ADAPTABILITY AND CUSTOMIZATION

The TEval framework is intentionally designed to be flexible and adaptable, accommodating a wide range of institutional types, roles, and teaching contexts. While the dimensions and criteria established within the framework are meant to represent essential elements of teaching quality, how they are interpreted, implemented, and weighted will vary depending on the local context of the institution or department. This adaptability is a key strength of the framework, allowing for what has been referred to as a "glocal" approach—one that balances global principles of teaching excellence with local needs and priorities.[5]

This adaptability is crucial in recognizing that while there are core principles that define high-quality teaching across disciplines and settings, the practical implementation of these principles can vary. (Chapters 3 and 4 will highlight some of these variations.) Different campuses—and often even departments within the same institution—can (and should) operationalize the framework in ways that align with their specific missions, student populations, and faculty roles.

For instance, one department may prioritize teaching practices that focus on problem-based learning, while another may emphasize mentoring and advising. The rubric provided by the TEval approach outlines core elements, such as defining dimensions of teaching practice and identifying forms of evidence to assess these practices, but leaves room for local customization in areas like defining and weighting of dimensions or the specific evidence collected.

Combining and Redefining Dimensions

While the TEval framework specifies seven dimensions of teaching, these are not fixed or prescriptive categories. Institutions and departments have the flexibility to combine, redefine, or create additional dimensions that better fit their specific educational goals. For example, at the University of Colorado Boulder (CU), some rubrics combined certain dimensions to better reflect the interdisciplinary teaching practices used in many of their programs. For example, in one department, the categories were established as: preparation for teaching (goals, selection of materials, approach), enactment of teaching (practices and climate), outcomes (achievement of learning goals, reflection and growth, professional development and contributions), and mentoring. Similarly, the University of California Los Angeles (UCLA), an institution that has adapted the TEval approach, has combined and redefined the seven TEval dimensions into just four. These examples illustrate how the framework can be adapted to meet specific needs while still maintaining a consistent emphasis on quality and evidence-based assessment.

Faculty Dialogues: Building Consensus and Buy-In

An essential aspect of implementing the TEval framework is engaging faculty in dialogues about the dimensions and criteria for evaluation. Faculty ownership of the process is critical for gaining widespread acceptance and ensuring that the evaluation system reflects shared values around teaching. As discussed in chapter 2, such dialogues often serve as a process of "sensemaking," where faculty collaboratively define what high-quality teaching looks like within their specific contexts and how it should be measured.

These conversations are not just a formality—they are central to building consensus and fostering a culture where continuous improvement in teaching is valued. At all of the institutions in the TEval project, this process has included formal workshops or retreats where faculty across departments have come together to discuss and refine the evaluation criteria. This kind of collaborative process not only ensures that the rubric reflects local teaching practices but also helps build a sense of collective responsibility for teaching excellence.

Local Autonomy: Determining Dimensions and Evidence

One of the critical decisions each institution or department faces when implementing the TEval framework is determining which dimensions of teaching to evaluate and which forms of evidence to collect. While the framework offers a set of recommended dimensions, such as "Achievement of Learning Outcomes" or "Class Climate," institutions have the autonomy to adapt these based on their priorities. For example, some institutions may choose to place more weight on dimensions related to out-of-classroom mentoring and advising, particularly in research-focused programs, while others may prioritize evidence of inclusive teaching practices and student engagement.

Similarly, the types of evidence collected can vary significantly. Some departments may rely heavily on peer observations and formal assessments, while others may incorporate student letters, focus group summaries, or reflections from the instructor as primary sources of evidence. The key is that each dimension is evaluated through multiple lenses, including self-assessment, student feedback, and third-party review, ensuring a holistic and valid evaluation process.

Overall Benefits for Faculty

As will be discussed in later chapters, one of the key benefits of the TEval framework is its emphasis on faculty development and continuous improvement. By involving faculty in the process of defining high-quality teaching and identifying the forms of evidence to be used, the framework fosters a culture of collaboration and shared responsibility. Faculty are not only evaluated but are given the tools and feedback necessary to improve their teaching over time. This developmental focus is a critical component of the TEval approach, ensuring that the evaluation process is not punitive but rather serves as a foundation for professional growth. In addition, the importance of an approach that addresses the documented and pervasive biases of end-of-term surveys cannot be overstated. Furthermore, when faculty work together to identify the components of their teaching practice that should be included in their evaluations, they can also consider how their work is aligned with institutional priorities. With many faculty experiencing the burnout that comes with too many responsibilities, opportunities to articulate the key elements of teaching may illuminate which responsibilities are essential (and, thus, should be valued, evaluated, and rewarded)—and which exceed reasonable expectations. Such conversations within departments may contribute to better working environments for all colleagues.

BROADER CONSIDERATIONS

The TEval approach offers a robust and flexible framework for evaluating teaching, but its implementation comes with broader considerations that require careful planning and reflection. While the framework aims to improve the depth and fairness of teaching evaluations, it also introduces complexities that institutions must address to ensure its success. We introduce these complexities here, but they are discussed in more detail in chapter 3, which focuses on the department as the location for much of the work of implementing change in teaching evaluation processes.

Time and Labor Considerations

As will be discussed in greater detail in chapter 3, one of the most significant challenges of implementing the TEval approach is the additional time and labor required from both faculty and departments when compared to using only an end-of-term student survey approach. Collecting, reviewing, and synthesizing multiple forms of evidence—ranging from syllabi and student work to peer observations and reflective narratives—takes more effort than distributing surveys that are electronically tabulated to produce a few numerical indicators.

Departments must be mindful of how they integrate this process into their existing workloads. Faculty, already stretched thin by their teaching, research, and service commitments, may find the additional burden of gathering evidence and participating in peer reviews daunting. Institutions should consider ways to alleviate some of this pressure by providing adequate time, resources, and support for faculty engaging in the evaluation process. Indeed, participating in the process as a reviewer should be recognized as a form of contribution to the educational mission of the department and institution. Additional support might include designating time for peer observations or compensating faculty for their contributions to the evaluation process. Perhaps the most effective approach is to design evaluation processes that align with and advance multiple departmental goals, ensuring that faculty time and effort serve several valuable purposes simultaneously.

Adapting the Framework to Local Contexts

As discussed above, a crucial aspect of the TEval approach is its adaptability, allowing departments to tailor the framework to their local context, institutional priorities, and specific teaching needs. Departments have the flexibility to redefine or combine the framework's dimensions in ways that better reflect their own values and teaching practices. Similarly, the forms of evidence collected can be adjusted to fit local circumstances, whether through peer observations, student feedback, or teaching-related publications.

Departments should engage in deliberate conversations about which elements of the framework to adopt, how to weigh different dimensions, and what forms of evidence will be most meaningful for their specific context. These decisions are not one-size-fits-all; they must reflect the unique goals and challenges of each institution. Some departments may prioritize inclusivity and student engagement, while others may focus on research mentoring or the integration of innovative teaching technologies. The TEval framework provides the flexibility to accommodate these diverse priorities, but departments must take ownership of the process to ensure that it aligns with their educational missions.

Deciding on the Scope of Holistic Evaluations

Another key consideration is how and when to incorporate holistic evaluations and for whom within a department. The TEval framework allows for flexibility in whether evaluations are conducted for all individuals each year or some individuals at key points in their careers. TEval focuses on evaluating an instructor's overall body of teaching work rather than an individual course (as is the case with student surveys of teaching). Therefore, institutions and departments can thoughtfully schedule evaluations at meaningful intervals rather than conducting them annually for every faculty member. This flexibility allows institutions or departments to create sustainable evaluation schedules that work with their available resources. This is useful because a holistic evaluation will likely require more time than is needed for the collection and analysis of quantitative end-of-term student surveys if they are the only means of evaluation. The focus on the instructor's body of work related to teaching, as opposed to an individual course, is particularly consequential in situations where a person's teaching spans multiple courses and types of responsibilities. An evaluation process may spotlight evidence from one course for a faculty member being evaluated or gather evidence from different courses in different semesters but combine this information when the holistic evaluation is completed.

An approach that helps distribute the work of holistic teaching evaluation is to develop a staggered timeline for the phase involving assembly and analysis of materials for particular individuals. Figure 1.3 demonstrates a timeline that allows for evaluating all members of a large department by staggering the years in which the evaluation is compiled for each person. In this example, there are three categories of individuals involved: *lecturers*, which can represent any type of instructional staff member not involved in the tenure track; *tenure-track*, representing those on the tenure track who have not yet achieved tenure; and *tenured*. Furthermore, the figure includes a tiered example for the *lecturers* in a situation where these individuals may have a contingent appointment for some periods of time followed by a continuing or longer-term appointment. The groups (Grp A, Grp B, etc.) at the beginning of each row are simply a way to break up each category of instructors into smaller numbers that can be evaluated in different years on a rotating basis.

The exact details of the examples in figure 1.3 should not be the focus for the reader. Instead, these are examples of ways to distribute the more work-intensive—and more informative—holistic evaluations over time so that they can have the greatest impact on the continuous improvement of faculty and educational success for students. If staggered evaluations (such as those in figure 1.3) would be useful to a department, that department should develop its own version, taking into account the types of instructional positions in that department, the number of individuals of each type, and the requirements of contracts in that context.

FIGURE 1.3 Examples of staggered timelines for carrying out holistic evaluations

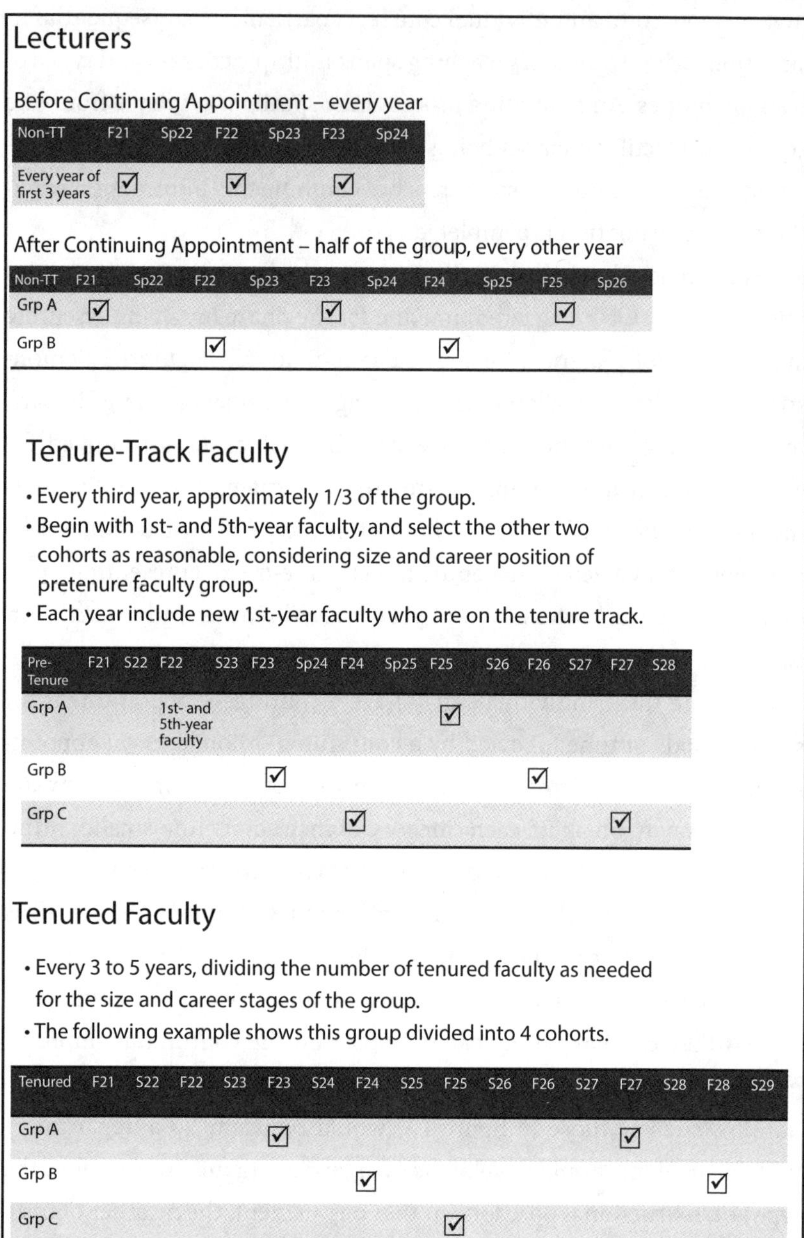

Lecturers

Before Continuing Appointment – every year

Non-TT	F21	Sp22	F22	Sp23	F23	Sp24
Every year of first 3 years	✓		✓		✓	

After Continuing Appointment – half of the group, every other year

Non-TT	F21	Sp22	F22	Sp23	F23	Sp24	F24	Sp25	F25	Sp26
Grp A	✓				✓				✓	
Grp B			✓				✓			

Tenure-Track Faculty

- Every third year, approximately 1/3 of the group.
- Begin with 1st- and 5th-year faculty, and select the other two cohorts as reasonable, considering size and career position of pretenure faculty group.
- Each year include new 1st-year faculty who are on the tenure track.

Pre-Tenure	F21	S22	F22	S23	F23	Sp24	F24	Sp25	F25	S26	F26	S27	F27	S28
Grp A			1st- and 5th-year faculty						✓					
Grp B					✓						✓			
Grp C							✓						✓	

Tenured Faculty

- Every 3 to 5 years, dividing the number of tenured faculty as needed for the size and career stages of the group.
- The following example shows this group divided into 4 cohorts.

Tenured	F21	S22	F22	S23	F23	S24	F24	S25	F25	S26	F26	S27	F27	S28	F28	S29
Grp A					✓								✓			
Grp B							✓								✓	
Grp C									✓							
Grp D											✓					

In many institutions, there are mandated points in time when comprehensive reviews must be carried out. In developing a timeline for holistic review, the timing of institutionally required reviews may be a useful benchmark to trigger holistic reviews. For example, it is possible to carry out the bulk of the holistic review in a different semester or academic year than the institutional comprehensive review is carried out and incorporate the earlier evaluation material.

Each department must decide which approach aligns best with its goals and institutional policies regarding the frequency of teaching evaluation. Holistic evaluations are particularly well-suited for formative purposes, where the emphasis is on faculty development and continuous improvement. In contrast, summative evaluations—typically used for decisions related to promotion, tenure, or contract renewal—might require holistic evaluations to take place at a specific point in time. Departments must consider whether their primary aim is to support faculty growth or to assess teaching outcomes for high-stakes decisions, or perhaps a combination of both.

Integration into Formative and Summative Evaluations

Finally, it is essential to consider how the TEval approach integrates into existing formative and summative evaluation processes. Formative evaluations, which are primarily aimed at supporting faculty development, may benefit from a more iterative and reflective use of the TEval framework. In this context, evaluations might emphasize dimensions such as "Reflection and Iterative Growth," providing faculty with feedback that can guide continuous improvement in their teaching. Summative evaluations, however, require a more structured and rigorous application of the framework, particularly when used for decisions related to tenure, promotion, or contract renewals. The flexibility of the TEval framework allows it to be adapted for use in both formative and summative evaluations. However, each department must make deliberate choices about how to implement it in these different contexts.

IMPORTANT POINTS TO TAKE FROM THIS CHAPTER

This chapter provides a comprehensive overview of the TEval approach and the ways it can transform the evaluation of teaching as a stepping stone to details that the following chapters will provide. Several key takeaways are essential for understanding this framework across diverse institutional contexts.

- *Holistic evaluation of teaching*: Unlike traditional end-of-term student surveys that focus on individual courses, the TEval approach emphasizes a comprehensive evaluation of an instructor's entire body of work related to teaching (with individual courses serving as exemplars). This includes elements of practice both inside and outside the classroom, offering a richer, more valid understanding of teaching effectiveness.
- *Multiple dimensions and forms of evidence*: The TEval framework evaluates teaching across multiple dimensions, such as teaching practices, student learning outcomes, and mentoring. Each dimension is supported by various forms of evidence—from syllabi and course materials to student feedback and peer reviews—ensuring a comprehensive and valid evaluation process. The use of multiple lenses and forms of evidence reduces bias and provides a more accurate assessment.
- *Adaptability and customization*: A core strength of the TEval framework is its adaptability. While the framework provides guiding dimensions for evaluating teaching, it allows for local customization to reflect the priorities, values, and teaching practices of individual departments and institutions. This flexibility ensures that the framework remains relevant to different contexts.
- *Collaborative faculty engagement*: Faculty ownership and participation in defining evaluation criteria are critical for the success of the TEval approach. The process encourages faculty to engage in meaningful

dialogues about what constitutes high-quality teaching, fostering a culture of collaboration and continuous improvement.

- *Local decision-making*: Departments have the autonomy to decide how to implement the TEval approach, including which dimensions to focus on, how to weigh them, and which forms of evidence to collect. This local decision-making ensures that the framework aligns with the unique goals and challenges of each institution, supporting a more tailored and relevant evaluation process.
- *Developmental focus on faculty growth*: A key benefit of the TEval framework is its emphasis on faculty development and continuous improvement. The evaluation process is designed not only to assess teaching performance but also to provide constructive feedback that helps instructors refine and improve their teaching practices over time.
- *Recognize that change takes time*: Implementing a holistic approach to teaching evaluation, as proposed by the TEval framework, is a long-term process. It requires patience, multiple iterations, and ongoing refinement. Small successes along the way should be celebrated, as they help maintain momentum and demonstrate the value of the changes being made. Leaders should expect adjustments and allow room for flexibility in the implementation.

In summary, the TEval approach offers a flexible, inclusive, and comprehensive framework for evaluating teaching. Its focus on holistic evaluation, adaptability, multiple forms of evidence, and faculty engagement ensures that teaching evaluation is not only fair and rigorous but also supportive of faculty development and educational excellence.

2

A Systemic Approach to Changing Teaching Evaluation

TRANSFORMING TEACHING EVALUATION IS a form of organizational change in higher education that requires a systemic approach. A systemic approach to change recognizes that higher education institutions are complex, dynamic systems composed of constantly interacting elements similar to ecosystems.[1] Like biological systems, universities have interrelated parts where what happens in one area affects another. In a biological system, a change in inputs (such as levels of rain or sun) affects the health of the plant or the quality of life within a lake. In a university or college, decisions and processes in one part of the organization, such as faculty governance, will help or hinder change efforts in other parts, such as academic departments. In the context of teaching evaluation, a college or university's evaluation and promotion system has multiple interwoven components. Changing how teaching is evaluated within departments has implications for the kinds of evidence that faculty will need to include in their promotion portfolios. Efforts to institute new processes and new kinds of evidence to assess a faculty member's effectiveness as a teacher need to be coordinated with the expectations of senior-level administrators or members of university-level promotion committees who will read and evaluate the promotion files.

At the same time, teaching evaluation can positively impact the system of educational practice in which it is embedded. By externalizing the values around educational practice that ought to take place, transformative teaching evaluations can inform elements of the system well beyond the individual faculty members, such as providing opportunities to advance public relations by making teaching excellence more visible and even contributing to fundraising and development. Systems approaches emphasize that a combination of elements within higher education institutions, such as supportive leadership, departmental conversations, professional development, and appropriate resources, create the fertile context for successful institutional change. Thus, changing teaching evaluation must be done with an eye toward the whole organizational system, including its culture, processes, leadership practices, and traditions.

This chapter provides an overview of how systemic and transformative change—the kind of change needed to advance significant transformation in teaching evaluation—occurs within the dynamic environment of a higher education institution. The first section of the chapter provides a conceptual overview of organizational change theories as they shed light on change in higher education institutions. The second part of the chapter presents several useful change frameworks that have been developed from research on specific change initiatives in higher education, such as projects to strengthen teaching and learning or to achieve greater inclusion and equity in higher education. These frameworks show how the theories can play out in comprehensive efforts to create measurable, impactful results in universities and colleges. The last section of the chapter draws from the theories and frameworks to zoom in on key elements of change processes: getting started, developing and implementing a set of complementary interventions and strategies to achieve the change goal, and ensuring the change initiative has long-term impact. Our goal in this chapter is to provide a foundation for the change approaches discussed in chapters 3 and 4, with chapter 3 addressing the critically important role of departments and department leaders in change processes to reform teaching evaluation and chapter 4 providing specific guidance for senior-level leaders, such as provosts and deans, who play an essential part in successful institutional change initiatives.

Our overview draws on the growing body of literature on organizational change in higher education. While the literature about organizational change in business and industry has some parallels with such research in higher education, universities and colleges are quite distinct from traditional forms of business and industry in terms of their goals, values, and working principles. For example, higher education institutions function with both bureaucratic and collegial systems, practice shared governance processes, honor faculty autonomy, and operate within complex ecosystems that include disciplinary associations, higher education organizations, government agencies, and funders.[2] For these reasons, we emphasize theoretical perspectives, research findings, frameworks, and principles for organizational change that are specifically relevant to higher education institutions.

THE RELEVANCE OF CHANGE THEORIES TO HIGHER EDUCATION

An overview of key ideas and theories about organizational change provides a foundation for discussing approaches to transforming teaching evaluation. One important concept is the notion of first-order change versus second-order change.[3] First-order change focuses on modest changes that can occur within the existing structure and work of an organization, often involving incremental and modest adjustments and improvements, but not requiring major shifts in the way the work is done or the underlying principles and assumptions guiding the work. In the organization development literature, this level of change usually involves what is called single-loop learning.[4] In a higher education organization, an example of first-order change would be reorganizing a university's admissions process to ensure that staff time is used as efficiently and effectively as possible and that student inquiries are fully addressed. On the other hand, second-order change involves deep, transformative shifts that require organizational members to rethink assumptions, norms, and structures and do their work in substantially new ways. Second-order change involves what has been called double-loop learning.[5] Change in teaching evaluation might occur as a first-order change, such as if the change were to require faculty members to provide examples of the materials they use for a teaching unit in addition to their student evaluation scores in their teaching review portfolios. However, the kind of transformation in teaching evaluation encouraged in this book is more likely to involve second-order change. That is, we are urging faculty members, department chairs, and senior institutional leaders to rethink what teaching evaluation means and why we do it, develop more comprehensive and holistic approaches, involve a greater range of stakeholders in the process, revise what is included in teaching evaluation portfolios, and use teaching evaluation processes as an avenue for deeper, more extensive, and more substantive discussion within departments of what high-quality teaching looks like and how it can be supported among colleagues. In other words, we are urging a rethinking of the values, norms, and processes related to teaching evaluation. This kind of work is transformative, second-order change. It can be challenging and demanding, but it also has the potential to have significant, meaningful, and long-lasting positive impact for students and faculty members.

Various change theories, each illuminating aspects of change within complex organizations, offer ideas that are relevant to higher education. Kezar has described several sets of theories (discussed below) that are particularly useful in higher education, explaining that "they can be understood as different layers of a complex process," each illuminating useful ideas and options for institutional leaders to consider as they work in their own contexts.[6] That is, change leaders need not select only one theory to guide their work. Rather, since different theories focus on different aspects of the change process, change leaders will find it useful to be familiar with and informed by ideas across several theories. We describe several of these sets of theories that are particularly useful for the higher education context.

Scientific management theories, like Kotter's theory of change, for example, have informed change work both in the business world and in the higher education sector.[7] These models emphasize top-down approaches and are sometimes critiqued as quite linear and, therefore, possibly less focused on organizational complexities and the diverse interests among organizational members (which is a hallmark of the culture in higher education). Nonetheless, these theories are useful in highlighting key elements of change that leaders should consider and in suggesting in what order. In the higher education context, scientific management theories draw attention to higher education organizations as purposeful and adaptive, they call for intentionality and rationality in change processes, and they encourage leaders to plan, set goals, and manage the change process by using such strategies as restructuring and offering relevant incentives.[8] Applying this perspective to an institutional initiative to rethink teaching evaluation, a provost, informed by scientific management theories, might consider what institutional policies would need to be adjusted if teaching evaluation processes were to change and on what timeline changes could realistically be made. For example, the faculty handbook might need to indicate different criteria for tenure packets; the tenure review committees at the department, college, and institutional levels would likely need new instructions for their work; and the timeline for substantive changes might need to be rolled out across several years.

Social cognition change theories provide a particularly compelling approach to change in higher education that emphasizes the importance of addressing the thinking of individuals involved in the change process.[9] That is, individuals need to interpret and make sense of the change goals, and often, the process requires a change in mindsets and collective schemas of understanding among those in the organization. Social cognition theories suggest that opportunities for conversation, collaboration, and communication can help foster change processes. For example, these approaches might take the form of facilitated interactions, departmental discussions, and institution-wide meetings to discuss aspects of change in teaching evaluation.

Cultural theories also recognize that organizational change cannot overlook the importance of addressing the underlying beliefs and values of organizational members.[10] These theories also emphasize that change processes must take into account and align with an organization's culture.[11] Change leaders need to find ways to help organizational members develop common meanings, understandings, and assumptions. Cultural theories highlight the usefulness of symbols, rituals, and ceremonies. Within colleges and universities, for example, department chairs and deans working to change teaching evaluation might use part of a faculty meeting to celebrate the work of a committee that had been considering how new approaches to teaching evaluation might be adapted to their departments.

Political theories emphasize that change processes often involve interactions and conflict among those with different interests.[12] Given the recognition of conflict as a normal part of change processes, this theoretical approach suggests that change leaders are wise to find allies, build coalitions and networks, and find ways to create collective understanding and vision about the change goals. In universities and colleges, this theoretical perspective might remind department leaders to find ways to bring together faculty members to discuss concerns about ideas to reform teaching evaluation in advance of any action or commitment. It might also guide institutional change leaders to consider the different groups to bring into the conversation about teaching evaluation, such as faculty governance groups, faculty unions, and councils of deans.

An evolutionary change perspective emphasizes taking a systems approach to change that recognizes the importance of the interactions between the organization and the environment.[13] This perspective emphasizes that a university or college is part of an ecosystem and that the pressures, resources, and challenges in the broader context have an impact on what occurs within the institution. Another set of theories relevant to higher education, called institutional and neoinstitutional theories, also emphasizes the interaction between organizations and their environments.[14] A particularly useful implication drawn from evolutionary and institutional theories is that the actions and interests of an organization's external constituencies can lend legitimacy and support to change initiatives within the organization.[15] As applied to transforming teaching evaluation, these theories remind institutional change leaders that their involvement in national discussions, conferences, or coalitions advancing ideas about why and how to change teaching evaluation can help them garner internal support. For example, a provost might send a team of deans, department chairs, and faculty members to a national meeting to learn how other institutions are thinking about teaching evaluation. The team's report back to the campus could help legitimize internal discussions and provide responses to those feeling concerned about or resistant to changing teaching evaluation.

Informed by these various theoretical approaches, Bolman and Deal provided a framework for examining and understanding organizations through four distinct frames or lenses: structural, human resources, political, and symbolic.[16] Each frame foregrounds an important dimension of organizations, and, thus, the frames can help change leaders reflect on what strategies or interventions would be most helpful in their context. The structural frame refers to the policies, rules and guidelines, and structural arrangements in an organization, while the human resources frame sheds light on the demographics, identities, experiences, and needs of the people in the organization. Focusing on another dimension of how an organization functions, the political frame highlights the importance and use of formal power and informal influence in organizational processes. Finally, the symbolic frame focuses attention on the cultural dimensions of the organization, including how meaning is conveyed and how culture and values affect behavior within the organization. Bolman and Deal's four-frame approach can be useful in a higher education context.[17] Specifically, considering the organization through each of the four frames enables change leaders to develop a comprehensive approach to planning possible change strategies. We find the Bolman and Deal framework especially helpful in highlighting different kinds of organizational change strategies and, thus, use it later in the chapter to provide practical guidance for leaders at various organizational levels as they select specific strategies to change teaching evaluation.

Applying Specific Change Frameworks in Higher Education

Theories of organizational change in higher education have been useful in the development of multiple frameworks that offer explicit and practical guidance and advice to change leaders. Here, we highlight several such frameworks that have emerged from research on projects organized to effect transformative change in universities and colleges and draw on multiple change theories. These frameworks are helpful sources of inspiration and ideas for institutional change leaders working on transforming teaching evaluation and other significant change goals.

The Association of American Universities (AAU) has provided the Framework for Systemic Change in Undergraduate STEM Education to provide guidance to institutional leaders fostering institution-wide education reform.[18] The framework emerged from a multi-institutional project through which the AAU helped universities increase the use of evidence-based instructional strategies known to improve teaching and learning in STEM fields. Central to the AAU framework is a commitment to reform education from a systemic view. The framework emphasizes three nested components: improving pedagogical practice, scaffolding faculty and student support as the change is implemented, and changing the culture within departments and the institution. While pedagogical change was the focus of the project that led to the development of this framework, one can easily imagine the transformation of teaching evaluation as a similar goal requiring a systemic approach.

The second element of this framework, scaffolding, refers to the support that is needed to incubate, implement, and sustain a pedagogical change, such as evidence-based teaching or more comprehensive, holistic teaching evaluation. The framework identifies several important types of scaffolding: professional development so that faculty can learn how to do what is being asked (whether it be new teaching methods or new approaches to teaching evaluation); resources, including tools and technology, that faculty can draw on to help implement the change; the collection and analysis of data that provide relevant measures of change and that assess progress toward achievement of a goal; and planning for physical facilities and space that provide support for the change goals (this element of scaffolding is less relevant to changing teaching evaluation processes than changing teaching practices themselves). The third element of the AAU framework focuses on cultural change, based on a recognition that transformational change requires systemic efforts within departments and the institution. One element of cultural change emphasized in this framework is the commitment of senior leaders, such as presidents and provosts, deans and department chairs, and faculty leaders. Developing measures to assess progress is another element of cultural change. In the AAU project, this included measures of departmental commitments to evidence-based teaching, measures of faculty teaching effectiveness beyond student ratings, and efforts to assess commitment to evidence-based teaching among faculty. Change leaders working on teaching evaluation would need to identify appropriate measures of progress. The AAU framework also emphasizes the importance of alignment of expectations, incentives, and rewards for faculty with the change goals.

Underlying the AAU framework is a recognition that systemic efforts to strengthen STEM teaching require long-term administrative support, including financial support; allocation of time and space; commitment to gather, analyze, and use data to support change work; and appropriate professional development. Overall, this framework reminds leaders that transformational change of teaching requires clear goals, practical scaffolding, and deep-level cultural change. Building on this AAU framework, members of the Roundtable on Systemic Change in Undergraduate STEM Education of the National Academies of Sciences, Engineering, and Medicine recently developed a Higher Education Instructional-Workforce Framework to help university and college leaders use three interdependent levers to foster change in teaching and learning.[19] These are professional development, academic governance, and faculty evaluation and reward systems, and they apply to faculty in all higher education institutions and positions.

The Keck/PKAL framework developed by Elrod and Kezar to explain change in higher education, particularly in undergraduate STEM education, uses a winding river as its metaphor.[20] Based on a project with eleven institutions in California working on improving undergraduate STEM education, this framework describes eight stages in change processes:

- Developing vision
- Reviewing the landscape and the capacity of the institution to engage successfully in the change process
- Identifying and analyzing challenges
- Choosing interventions and strategies
- Determining institutional readiness for action
- Implementing plans
- Measuring results
- Dissemination and planning for next steps

The model emphasizes the importance of a vision developed by a team of diverse voices that articulates clear goals, outcomes, and measures of progress and aligns with institutional priorities. The authors remind change leaders that developing a vision should involve an analysis of the institutional landscape. That takes time, particularly to secure sufficient buy-in from members of the institution. The authors also enumerate the multiple barriers that thwart or challenge change processes. Such barriers include lack of attention to examining implicit assumptions about the problem to be addressed, underlying beliefs and biases among faculty that may not align with the change goals and process, inadequate planning and incentives to secure faculty involvement, leadership turnover, and shifts in the composition of the team coordinating the change. The river metaphor highlights the dynamic, emergent nature of a change process, the challenges and obstacles that can pop up and thwart or delay the process, and the multiple entry and exit paths possible for institutional participants. While emphasizing an overall trajectory of change, the metaphor also captures the dynamic recirculation zones and feedback loops that can occur, which means the path is not simply linear. In short, complexities are to be expected as institutions embark on transformative change.

Through a study of more than twenty universities that have received grants through the National Science Foundation's ADVANCE program, Laursen and Austin created a framework that identifies several sets of change levers.[21] Recognizing that women and faculty of color have faced challenges in academic organizations, the NSF ADVANCE program supports universities in creating more diverse, inclusive, and equitable work environments. A principle of the change work in this program is to "fix the system, not the women." Like the other frameworks discussed in this chapter, Laursen and Austin's framework focuses on systemic change.[22] Their change framework for creating more inclusive higher education highlights twelve interventions organized into four categories: interrupting biased processes, rebooting workplaces, supporting the whole person, and fostering individual success. It also provides steps that can draw on these interventions: identifying and framing the problem, analyzing the context, choosing the strategies and interventions, and emphasizing key "anchoring strategies" for change (i.e., managing implicit bias, ensuring strong leadership, recognizing the importance of the department, and establishing a strategic approach to communication). The framework also identifies elements to include in implementation efforts: ensuring the involvement of committed leaders; establishing buy-in, identifying allies, and communicating effectively; tracking, monitoring, and evaluating the change process; and sustaining change over time.

Henderson, Beach, and Finkelstein offered another useful framework in their analysis of several hundred publications documenting undergraduate STEM education transformation in the United States (spanning 1995–2008).[23] Their research resulted in a typology of change strategies organized into four areas: disseminating curriculum and pedagogy, developing reflective teachers, enacting policy, and developing a shared vision. They emphasized that effective change initiatives require understanding higher education institutions as complex systems and designing change strategies appropriate for the specific system. The importance of taking a systems perspective in designing change initiatives appears in several other theories and frameworks discussed in this chapter and again in the next two chapters focused on guidance for department chairs (chapter 3) and senior institutional leaders (chapter 4) seeking to advance reform in teaching evaluation.

These frameworks offer change leaders in higher education practical guidance for designing and implementing transformative change initiatives. We also recommend several toolkits that align with the principles in these frameworks and can help change leaders and institutional planning teams. In particular, Elrod and Kezar's *Change Leader Toolkit 2.0* offers a straightforward and practical guide for presidents, deans, and department chairs to use as they help advance their institutions toward significant change goals.[24] The toolkit helps facilitate conversation among leaders and working groups strategizing about change initiatives in their own institutions. We also want to call attention to the increasing interest in addressing equity as part of any change process in higher education. In addition, the American Council on Education (ACE), in collaboration with the Pullias Center for Higher Education at the University of Southern California, offers a range of useful resources to support shared equity leadership, available on the ACE website.[25] Given that efforts to transform teaching evaluation align with and support institutional commitments to treat faculty justly and to create learning environments that more equitably meet the needs of all students, the ACE/Pullias resources may also offer ideas and practical strategies for ensuring that change work models equitable practices and advances greater equity in institutions.

KEY PRINCIPLES IN THE CHANGE PROCESS

Our intent in the discussion above has been to show that decisions about how to advance change can be guided by extensive research on how organizations (especially higher education organizations) work and change. In this section, we draw on this theoretical and research background to provide practical guidance for higher education leaders. This last section of this chapter draws from organizational change theories and frameworks to focus on specific principles related to effective change processes. We have organized this discussion into three sections that acknowledge the practical issues confronting change leaders: getting started, selecting and implementing interventions and strategies, and sustaining change and building for the long haul. In subsequent chapters, we take the discussion of key principles further by addressing how department chairs (chapter 3) and senior-level institutional leaders (chapter 4) can advance and support change efforts to transform teaching evaluation.

Getting Started: Initiating a Change Process in Higher Education

This section on initiating a transformative change process urges leaders to consider three related topics at the start of a project: assessing institutional readiness to change; examining institutional culture and context; and designing a combined top-down, bottom-up, and middle-out approach to transformative change. Considering and addressing these three features of change will very likely occur simultaneously.

Assessing Institutional Readiness to Change

As a university or college considers an effort to change its approach to teaching evaluation, early discussion should focus on the institution's readiness to change.[26] Organizations are always developing and changing, and thus, they are at different levels of readiness to engage in a change process. Some aspects of readiness need to be considered regardless of an initiative's focus. These include the institution's overall health, the internal or external pressures confronting the institution, and the timing of the intended change project. If a university is facing a financial crisis or extensive turnover of senior leaders, administrative and faculty leaders may have little time or energy for a project to change teaching evaluation. On the other hand, an effort to change teaching evaluation may be a timely way to address institutional challenges and opportunities related to student success or the needs of a diversifying population of faculty and students. In preparing for any change initiative, leaders must consider the institution's mission, structures, governance processes, technologies, human infrastructure, and communication practices in regard to how they will help or thwart the change work.[27]

Considering institutional readiness to change also means looking specifically at organizational characteristics and factors that are directly relevant to a specific change goal. As discussed in chapters 3 and 4, change leaders should consider the mission and value priorities of the department or institution and the extent to which the change goal is aligned with and relevant to those key organizational characteristics. Other necessary conditions that relate to institutional readiness to engage in a transformational change process around teaching evaluation include the following:

- A sufficient level of support, interest, and commitment from institutional leaders at various organizational levels, including central administrators, teaching center leaders, deans, and department chairs.
- An institutional infrastructure to support departments engaged in changing their approaches to teaching evaluation. This might include a centralized unit such as a teaching center as well as supportive and interested colleagues who have expertise in evaluating teaching.
- Openness among administrative leaders and faculty committees to consider new approaches to evaluating faculty work.
- Interest among faculty members to invest time in learning about and working on the improvement of teaching evaluation.

Examining Institutional Culture and Context

Achieving significant change in complex organizations is always challenging, but progress and success are more likely if leaders have considered the specific context and culture of the institution.[28] Context includes such things as university norms, governance structures, and history. General principles for effecting change are relevant across contexts, but institutional leaders who develop their plans based on analysis of their specific institutional environment are more likely to succeed.

The leaders of the TEval projects at the University of Colorado Boulder (CU), University of Kansas (KU), and University of Massachusetts Amherst (UMass) have had similar goals to change teaching evaluation, yet each has been sensitive and responsive to their specific institutional contexts. Each institution's culture and history have influenced which approaches and strategies have been most feasible for advancing change in teaching evaluation. For example, with its history of extensive departmental involvement in teaching improvement projects facilitated by its Center for Teaching Excellence (CTE), change leaders at KU strategically situated their teaching evaluation project within the center's purview. At the same time, the vice provost for faculty affairs recognized the value of linking the TEval work with institutional efforts to improve promotion processes. The TEval change leader at CU, well-respected as a faculty leader, recognized the existing work of departmental action teams in improving teaching practice and decided to use the same approach with change efforts around teaching evaluation. The CU TEval change leader also recognized that the deans of several colleges would be key partners in changing teaching evaluation at an institution that, at the time, did not have a well-established teaching center. At UMass, where decentralization and faculty collective bargaining shape the culture, the associate dean serving as the TEval change leader needed to rely on departmental interest, commitment, and autonomy to advance change in teaching evaluation. Not all change efforts move up from the departments, however. For instance, at another university that has recently transformed teaching evaluation (although not part of the TEval project), a vice provost identified departments ready for change, engaged the support of the provost, and only then encouraged departments to get involved.

Each approach reflects the particular institutional context, including history with change efforts related to teaching and learning, the level of interest among provosts and deans, the extent of departmental commitment and leadership regarding changing teaching evaluation, and practices around departmental autonomy. The overarching principle is that institutional leaders seeking to support or initiate efforts to change teaching evaluation need to assess the context and culture at their institution to decide what approaches would be most feasible. The issues mentioned in the discussion of institutional readiness are important in assessing what change processes and strategies will be most appropriate in the specific institutional context. Additionally, these aspects of the context are especially important to consider as a change project begins:

- The level of institutional interest in, commitment to, and organizational space for the change project.
- The interest of administrative and faculty leaders in taking on responsibilities and investing time in the change process, the potential influence and impact they might have, and their knowledge about effective teaching evaluation.
- The presence (or not) of a well-respected teaching center interested in working on teaching evaluation and the history of departmental collaboration and work with such a center.
- The resources available to support departmental change work. This includes consultants who can offer ideas about alternative approaches to teaching evaluation or facilitators who can help lead departmental meetings on changes to teaching evaluation.
- The traditions of faculty involvement and experience in enacting institutional change, including the extent of centralization versus decentralization in institutional decision-making processes.
- The presence of faculty-based unionized bargaining units and how they will want and need to be involved.
- The availability of resources, tools, and training, either within the institution or through national conferences, networks, and associations, to support the change initiative.

Taking a Top-Down, Bottom-Up, Middle-Out Approach to Transformative Change

Another issue to consider early in the process of initiating transformative change is where the leadership for the work is situated. Transformative change in teaching evaluation must situate the work within several levels of the organization, including top-down, bottom-up, and middle-out involvement.[29] For middle and larger-scale institutions, changes need to be situated primarily within departments, as much of the work of evaluating faculty teaching occurs there; thus, faculty members and department chairs must be involved. However, making institution-wide changes in how faculty are evaluated also requires the support and involvement of senior leaders, such as deans and provosts, as well as faculty involved in institutional governing bodies, such as senates and institution-level governing and policy committees.

At mid-size to large-scale universities and colleges, departments and academic units are often the key areas for leading and sustaining change work. At other types of institutions, such as liberal arts colleges, community colleges, and regional institutions, the college, school, or division may be a more appropriate locus for efforts to change teaching evaluation. Those are the places where teaching assignments are made, policies developed, and norms of practice established.[30] Values around teaching emerge within disciplinary and departmental contexts, where those values influence how faculty teach, allocate their time to different dimensions of academic work, and value teaching. Faculty are hired into and usually strongly identify with the academic unit. Evaluations are typically conducted within academic units by peers who collect and interpret relevant data and make assessments and decisions about promotion. Because so much of faculty work, including teaching, is organized around the department, it is the logical home base for initiating reform in teaching evaluation. In the project described in this book, change leaders at each of the three participating institutions identified a set of departments interested in and ready to reform teaching evaluation. In the next chapter, we discuss the approaches those departments used.

While the department is likely to be the primary location of efforts to change teaching evaluation, it is not the only location. As emphasized at the outset of this chapter, because universities and colleges are complex organizational systems, changes in approaches to evaluating teaching also involve other levels and stakeholders in the institution. If a department is situated within a college, the dean will need to agree to the changes, and any college-level committee that reviews promotion materials will need to agree to use any new forms of evaluation evidence that they will receive. Changes in one department are likely to raise interest or questions in other departments since deans or college-wide review committees typically expect faculty promotion and review materials to be organized in parallel fashion across departments. Similar issues will arise at the institution level. A provost or university-wide review committee for promotion may expect all units to follow similar guidelines and processes; thus, change in one unit may have a ripple effect across the institution. Furthermore, institutional policies and practices embedded in the organization over time may constrain how a department considers options in its approach to changing teaching evaluation.

Because efforts to create transformative change at a university or college have implications across the institution, leadership in support of the change is needed at multiple levels. Those working at the grassroots or bottom-up level (faculty members) and the middle level (department chairs and deans) can envision and nurture interest in changing teaching evaluation. They develop local plans, encourage colleagues to be supportive and involved (or at least not resistant), and implement new ideas. However, their efforts need to be in concert with the priorities and perspectives of leaders higher in the organizational structure, such as deans, provosts, vice provosts, faculty union leaders, and other institutional policy makers. While a dean or provost could decide unilaterally to change teaching evaluation expectations and processes, they would very likely run into barriers and resistance without the interest and agreement of at least some grassroots and middle-level leaders (either administrative leaders or faculty leaders) at the department level. Furthermore, mid-level institutional leaders, such as teaching center directors, need to be included, as they often help to manage and mediate the work, perspectives, and issues that arise as grassroots leaders and institutional leaders engage around a change project.

Each institution we have studied has involved leaders at various levels in carrying out change processes, although the patterns of leadership vary by institution. For example, the change process at CU involved a strong faculty leader, change facilitators who worked closely with interested departments, and several deans who committed their colleges' departments to become involved. At KU, the leaders of the Center for Teaching Excellence were key institutional leaders, supporting departmental change teams. The interest and support of a vice provost also helped integrate the departmental work on teaching evaluation into institutional policies. At UMass, faculty leadership within departments was a key factor, with important support articulated by faculty union leaders.

Other universities and colleges considering a change in teaching evaluation should consider what and where in the institution leadership can be tapped—who is respected, who has informal or formal influence, and what existing relationships can be the foundation for the work. If an institutional teaching center has a reputation for doing effective and respected work with faculty members and departments, it may have the informal influence and goodwill to attract departmental leaders and bring together faculty teams. If strong interest from senior leaders is not apparent and a well-regarded teaching center is not available, an enthusiastic faculty leader can potentially inspire other leaders, such as deans, to get involved and encourage others. At some institutions, a faculty union may be a strong ally for effecting change in teaching evaluation. Effective change processes draw from formal and informal leadership to create bottom-up, middle-out, and top-down support for the change process. In chapter 3, we discuss more fully what kind of departmental work, involving faculty and department leaders, advances change in teaching evaluation. Then, in chapter 4, we offer specific ideas for provosts, deans, teaching center directors, and others in senior-level leadership positions.

Selecting and Implementing Change Interventions and Strategies

Once institutional readiness is assessed and the unique aspects of the institution are recognized, change leaders need to consider what strategies will be useful to accomplish the change goal. This section discusses how to think about selecting strategies for working on the reform of teaching evaluation at the department and institution levels. First, we explain a framework that can help generate ideas for a comprehensive and integrated set of strategies, and then we discuss specific strategies especially relevant to reforming teaching evaluation.

Developing a Set of Multiple, Integrated Strategies to Advance Change

An accumulation of evidence shows that systemic change in complex organizations, such as universities and colleges, requires multiple strategies used at different times and at multiple levels of the organization.[31] That is, a single strategy or intervention to advance change in teaching evaluation is unlikely to be sufficiently effective. For example, providing departments and their faculty with examples of more comprehensive, holistic approaches to teaching evaluation will be helpful, but generally will be far from sufficient to actually motivate them to change. Faculty are likely to be concerned with a number of issues—the time they would need to invest in changing the evaluation process in their department and whether it would "count" in their work assignments; the norms within the institution that privilege the way evaluation has occurred for many years; the way college- and institution-level promotion committees might scrutinize new departmental approaches to evaluation; and the approaches peer institutions are taking in evaluating teaching. In other words, change requires consideration of many aspects of how faculty work is done and how the organization works at the department, college, and institutional levels. Change requires multiple levers, or interventions, at multiple levels of the institution. Furthermore, different levers may be important at different stages of the change process; and, as discussed, leaders at different levels may be important at different times in the process. For example, at the start of a change process, explicit encouragement from a department chair or dean may motivate faculty members to become involved in rethinking teaching evaluation. Once a new approach has been envisioned, securing the support of the college or university promotion committees and their faculty leaders may become particularly helpful.

As discussed above, various theories have practical implications for higher education practice. We have found that Bolman and Deal's four-frame approach provides an especially helpful framework for leaders when they are at the point of identifying and selecting useful practical strategies for advancing a change goal.[32] Thus, in this section, we use the frames in the Bolman and Deal approach to organize our discussion of specific strategies for changing teaching evaluation.

Strategies for Change Related to Organizational Structures

The structural frame draws consideration to the policies, rules and guidelines, and structural arrangements in an organization. Examining a university or college through the structural frame focuses on the importance of organizational policies and practices, such as an institution's processes for annual professional evaluation and promotion decisions. In efforts to change teaching evaluation, the structural frame highlights the department as the primary location where teaching evaluation is conducted. For this reason, the TEval project situated change work primarily within departments. At CU, change facilitators worked closely with faculty interested in teaching evaluation in departments and provided regular guidance based on the needs and questions within those departments. Explicit attention to the departmental structure (and the need for enhanced structures to enact change) was a core strategy that led to significant success at CU. Similarly, UMass and KU also focused on supporting departmental work as central to changing teaching evaluation. At UMass, the associate dean facilitating the change process met regularly with participating departments to provide suggestions. At KU, the Center for Teaching Excellence had a strong record of encouraging change around teaching by working with departmental teams. Center leaders followed a similar approach with TEval, inviting faculty teams and chairs to join the project.

The structural frame also draws attention to an institution's formal policies and practices. Any plans to create more holistic, comprehensive evaluations of teaching must align with policies at the department, college, and institutional levels for how faculty are evaluated for personnel and salary decisions and the content of promotion portfolios. Thus, one strategy to support change is to engage the committee members who will review portfolios in discussion of why changes in teaching evaluation are needed, what evidence might be expected with more comprehensive teaching evaluation, and what criteria might be used in evaluating new kinds of portfolios submitted for review. Furthermore, a university might need to change its technical guidelines for the length of portfolios or the expected content of summary essays in which faculty explain their approach to teaching and the evidence they are providing. Faculty members will also want to know whether their department chairs will "count" time spent on departmental committees to change teaching evaluation in annual reviews and considerations for salary allocations. Preparing evaluation committees and ensuring the alignment of the faculty reward system with new approaches to teaching evaluation are key strategies for structural change.

Strategies for Change Related to the Human Resources Frame

When leaders consider the organizational change process through the human resources frame, they look at the demographics, identities, experiences, and needs of the people in the organization. To effect transformative change, faculty must be engaged and interested, as expressed through willingness to invest time in departmental and institutional committees to plan the change and to incorporate it into their own work and experiences. Faculty involvement is essential in "bottom-up" support for the change goal. As discussed earlier, the social cognition theories of organizational change emphasize that individuals need to understand and value the proposed change. Faculty members' existing mental schemas may be in conflict or dissonance with proposed new ideas, creating challenges to the change process.[33] "Sense-making" and "sense-giving" are important parts of the process that help individuals feel engaged and supported in a change process.[34] Sense-making is the process through which individuals come to understand what the change is about. It involves grappling with relevant prior ideas they might have held. Sense-giving is the process through which individuals communicate with others about the change goals. Some faculty members participate in learning communities or "communities of transformation" in which they interact with colleagues to learn about, make sense of new approaches to teaching, and work through their mental models and related assumptions.[35] These communities have been found to be quite helpful in supporting faculty members engaged in change efforts. In addition to highlighting the importance of such spaces for mutual learning, the human resource frame also reminds change leaders that when organizational members are asked to engage in a change process, they need appropriate information to understand and take action. Providing access to examples and cases can be a useful strategy.

Practical strategies informed by the human resources frame to support transformational change include opportunities for conversations and workshops among organizational members and stakeholders and occasions to review and discuss resources and examples. When faculty members work in groups in their departments to discuss their ideas about what represents effective teaching in their fields and how to change teaching evaluation, they engage in sense-making and sense-giving. Also, when they have access to examples of what a revised approach to teaching evaluation might look like, rubrics to use for observing peers or reflecting on one's teaching, and comparative examples from the work of other departments or institutions, they are receiving information that helps them expand and change their thinking, create new mental models, and address any dissonance in their thinking. Similarly, leaders and members of promotion committees also need opportunities to create new mental models of what effective teaching looks like, how it can be represented to others, and how it can be evaluated more effectively.

The case study institutions provide excellent examples of ways to provide such support for faculty members. Each case university encouraged participating departments to create faculty teams to work together over time to discuss what characterizes excellent teaching in their particular field, what evidence would be appropriate to demonstrate effective teaching, and how change in teaching evaluation could best occur in the specific departmental context. This kind of work among a group of faculty constitutes a sense-making and sense-giving process. The teaching center at KU regularly arranged conversations among teams from departments working on teaching evaluation, enabling them to share lessons about the change process, discuss challenges, and create new understandings about teaching evaluation. All three institutions participated in periodic national meetings at which faculty and administrative representatives from the three institutions convened to share information about progress, effective levers for change, and emergent challenges. Participants provided positive feedback about the benefits of facilitated conversations in which ideas, resources, and concerns were discussed in a cross-institutional context. Departmental working groups, learning communities, and cross-unit and cross-institutional conversations are effective strategies that enable the sense-making that fosters change.

In addition to managing their assumptions and understandings, participants in change processes need information and ideas of what is possible. Thus, in addition to encouraging a variety of conversations and workshops, institutional change leaders in the three case institutions also provided resources and examples. These included information on how different departments tested new evaluation processes (for example, some departments incorporated new approaches to teaching evaluation into their expectations for teaching assistants, and others focused initially on the annual review process for pretenure faculty). CU provided change facilitators to lead department-level faculty work sessions, thus ensuring departments had specific information needed at each stage of their work. Across the TEval project, the change leaders at each institution provided sample rubrics, guidelines developed to help departmental conversations, and compelling examples of departmental experiments. The availability of such professional development opportunities is essential in change work. These sessions help individuals engage in necessary sense-making, ensure participants that change goals are realistic and can be accomplished, and reduce the time needed to advance the change.

Strategies for Change Related to the Political Frame

The political frame emphasizes the importance and use of formal power and informal influence in organizational processes. This frame is also a reminder to include in decision-making processes the people who have the power and influence to provide support and resources. For example, in a university or college, significant change in how teaching is evaluated will require the agreement and support of faculty members, department chairs and deans, and those on committees that assess faculty work and quality. It will often benefit from the support of teaching center staff who can provide relevant professional development. The political frame also highlights the importance of allies within change processes. Allies may be groups or individuals with related, although not necessarily the same, goals and interests, and, thus, who may be able to help advance the change goal. Another dimension of the political frame pertains to resources. Change leaders must have sufficient access to necessary resources, including fiscal resources, time, and the expertise of human resources to carry out the work. Senior leaders are often needed as allies to ensure that schools and departments are supported in allocating their time to the change work and securing any necessary help.

Institutional leaders should identify helpful participants or allies in efforts to transform teaching evaluation. These include deans, department chairs, members of college and institutional review committees, teaching center colleagues, and students, all of whom have the potential to support or impede the process of change. Effective strategies include informing these stakeholders (potential allies) of the change goal and explaining why it is important to the institution, how it relates to institutional priorities, and why it is relevant to the interests of the potential ally.

The case institutions include several examples of how allies can be involved in efforts to transform teaching evaluation. At UMass, the faculty union had a longstanding interest in ensuring equity in faculty evaluation processes. In this context, the union stood as a voice of support for department-level work to create more holistic, transparent, and equitable approaches to teaching evaluation. At KU, the vice provost for faculty affairs saw ways to connect the teaching center's work on evaluation with other institutional discussions about defining and evaluating faculty work and revising student surveys of teaching. This interest from the provost's office added further support and recognition to the work. The faculty change leader at CU recognized the importance of support from senior-level administrative leaders. Thus, he ensured recognition and endorsement from the provost. Additionally, he connected with several deans to ensure they were familiar with the work underway in a number of departments and helped them see how more effective teaching evaluation related to institutional goals around excellence and quality. Securing the interest and commitment of several deans led to more departmental involvement across the institution and more extensive support for the change goal. Each of these examples is evidence of why change leaders should analyze who might be effective allies and invest time in informing, cultivating, and securing their support. (Later in this chapter, we also discuss the benefits of connections beyond the institution.)

Strategies for Change Related to the Symbolic Frame

The cultural dimensions of the organization are the central focus of the symbolic frame. Fostering a shared vision and narrative is a key part of the symbolic dimensions of a change process.[36] Provosts, deans, and department chairs play a central role in creating a narrative about the change goal and ensuring it is shared widely. Successful change processes involve creating clear communication about the change goals, ensuring the goals are aligned with institutional values and priorities, and celebrating progress toward achievement of the goals. Changes in teaching evaluation that are antithetical to institutional values about faculty work will be difficult to advance. For example, if institutional culture and norms privilege research accomplishments over teaching, faculty may be skeptical that efforts to create more holistic, transparent, and equitable teaching evaluation are genuine or likely to succeed. Unless explicit messaging emphasizes that teaching is a valued activity, faculty will stay with long-held, historically-based perceptions that research is more valued than teaching.

Establishing a variety of communication strategies is another element in managing the symbolic aspect of organizational change. Those in leadership roles sometimes assume that a statement about an institutional project or goal is quickly understood and incorporated into the work of organizational members. In actuality, leaders often need to repeat messages frequently and find ways to express key ideas in multiple venues and forms.[37] Practical ways to convey messages about change goals, foster wide understanding and buy-in, and invite participation include written messages from leaders, periodic newsletters, and websites where more extensive information and links can be provided. Change leaders can be explicit about how a change initiative directly contributes to stated institutional priorities by naming a specific priority in a strategic plan and explaining how the change effort advances that priority and can lend credibility and legitimacy to a project. Inviting governance bodies, such as university committees on faculty affairs or tenure, to discuss and offer advice about the change goals can create allies while also inserting information about the change project into the discussion and minutes of committee meetings. Asking provosts to include discussion of the change initiative in regular deans' council agendas symbolically shows the importance of the work and encourages deans to be supportive and involved. At most universities and colleges, provosts and deans have annual meetings to discuss tenure and promotion cases. At those meetings, a provost's questions about how teaching evaluation is changing and becoming more equitable, transparent, and reflective sends a critical message about the importance of transforming teaching evaluation.

An important and sometimes overlooked symbolic lever for change is the use of celebrations and public recognition. Major change initiatives can take considerable time, and delays or setbacks are common. One way to keep the initiative moving forward is by planning periodic celebrations and acknowledging efforts and people. Individuals who are investing time and serving as change leaders should be recognized for their service. Hard work conducted over time can be challenging and deserves appreciation from colleagues and leaders. Perhaps of even more importance are occasional celebrations that remind the institution and all its members of the progress being made. Taking time to recognize benchmarks on the way to institution-wide change in teaching evaluation can help maintain energy and commitment and inspire the involvement of others. Recognition and celebration can occur in various forms, including comments of appreciation in faculty meetings that recognize leadership and time spent on a project, articles in campus publications, occasional informal lunches or off-campus gatherings in honor of progress made, and full-scale luncheons or dinners that convene all those involved in a change initiative.

KU provides a good example of how to use symbolic elements to foster interest and involvement in a change initiative. The leadership of the Center for Teaching Excellence in collaborative projects involving departmental teams to improve teaching was widely appreciated and respected.

As the TEval project began, change leaders at KU subtly reminded departments how much they had enjoyed and learned from previous collaborative change projects. Essentially, the change leaders were building on the goodwill, success, and meaning-making that had occurred in the earlier projects as encouragement for departments to engage with the new change work. At each of the three institutions involved in TEval, the imprimatur of the National Science Foundation (which funded the cross-institutional project) also provided an important symbolic message about the importance of transforming teaching evaluation. Senior institutional leaders, deans, and department chairs frequently mentioned that they appreciated having their institution selected to be part of an important national effort. Similarly, alignment and participation with larger national efforts, such as those of the National Academies of Sciences, Engineering, and Medicine and the Association of American Universities, provide credibility and recognition of the important work on campuses. As discussed later in the chapter, securing support and recognition from well-respected groups external to the institution is a powerful lever supporting a change initiative.

Sustaining Change and Building for the Long Haul

The term *institutionalization* is often used to represent the ultimate goal of a change initiative. This term usually means that the change goal has become widespread, permanent, codified in policy, and routine in the life of the institution.[38] Some theorists identify broad stages in a change process, including mobilization, implementation, and institutionalization.[39] In a project aiming to transform teaching evaluation, the long-term goal is likely to be institution-wide use of a more substantive approach to evaluation. That goal is important, but the path to achieving it may mean that some departments establish more effective approaches before others do. Finding ways to maintain momentum is necessary, even in the face of unexpected issues that require organizational attention. Ultimately, the goal should be commitment to continuous improvement, including regularly revisiting, updating, and modernizing our approaches to match the changing landscape of higher education and our learners. This final section of the chapter discusses three ways to maintain momentum and support the university or college as efforts to transform teaching evaluation move toward full institutionalization: monitoring and evaluation; handling resistance, barriers, and threats; and connecting with external partners.

Continuous Monitoring, Evaluation, and Improvement

An important principle in organizational change is to use data at all stages in a process and to engage in continuous monitoring, tracking, and evaluation. Attention to data and evidence is critical in helping change efforts take root and embed deeply into an institution's culture. Data can help frame initial plans for a change process by deepening understanding of a problem to be addressed. As a change effort continues, leaders can establish benchmarks for monitoring what the process is achieving, what challenges or barriers are emerging, what evidence of success can be celebrated, and what issues need attention and improvement. Change leaders at all levels—senior leaders, department leaders, and faculty leaders—have contributions to make in discussions of appropriate benchmarks. Formative assessment helps those working on the change process keep an eye on what is happening so they can adjust the course and address concerns as they arise. Summative evaluation emphasizes benchmarks at certain points in the process, asking how much has been accomplished to date. Periodic summative assessment helps leaders keep the change initiative visible to institutional members and provides specific moments to look back at accomplishments and to look forward to next steps. Both formative and summative assessments are important to institutionalizing change goals, and both rely on gathering evidence about the change process and the impact of the change work.

A long history of research and practice in both management and education has created considerable knowledge about the use of data and assessment practices. One key idea from management is that change should be organized around measurable objectives. Drucker encouraged identifying specific goals, communicating them to employees, designing specific performance measures linked with incentives for achievement, and using data to guide continuous improvement.[40] Kotter, whose work has guided change efforts in both business and education, recognized the importance of creating short cycles of change where outcomes could be measured and used to motivate continued work.[41] In the health fields, the ideas of improvement science have called attention to using focused, data-driven interventions that move the field toward more effective practices.[42] These ideas about strategies to improve quality have also been applied in education settings in the form of networked improvement communities, or NICs.[43] This approach involves multiple organizations (such as universities) or departments working on a common problem and engaging in multiple rounds of change strategies, sharing knowledge, data, and analysis of the impact and outcomes of their work, and then determining steps to move forward. In higher education, recognition of the importance of using data and ongoing evaluation has gained traction in recent years, as shown in the growing interest in data analytics as a tool for tracking student learning and identifying specific courses and programs where interventions may be most effective.

In projects focused on transforming teaching evaluation, data-informed monitoring, tracking, and assessing should occur from the start. As change agents initiate discussion about teaching evaluation, they can gather both anecdotes and systematic data about what issues are concerning their colleagues. This information can help define a specific change goal. As projects get underway, leaders can decide on benchmarks that will show progress, and they can provide opportunities for those involved in the process to discuss their work. Data and information can be used to plan and improve change strategies; gather information about what is working and what is not; identify which departments are making progress and might be exemplars for other departments; reveal institutional policies, structures, or processes that hinder or improve the process; and remind change leaders of what deserves celebration. Other useful questions to explore include who is involved and who is not, what progress is being made across the institution, what challenges or barriers are emerging, what strategies are particularly effective, and what outcomes have been achieved.

Various types of data can be used to monitor, track, and assess progress for a change project. Strategies useful to provide formative feedback include case studies of specific departments; interviews with faculty, department chairs, and leaders of committees involved in the process; surveys of faculty or others; and documents produced as part of the effort. In the TEval project, an outside researcher (one of this book's coauthors) visited the three case institutions regularly to interview, observe, and learn what was happening with the change efforts. The data were analyzed and syntheses provided to the change leaders to use in working with departments and institutional leaders. Discussions among the institutional change leaders enabled the exchange of useful ideas, as did periodic meetings of faculty and other participants from across the institutions. External evaluators can be particularly helpful in identifying issues not as visible to those embedded in the institution or asking questions that may be less comfortable for those within the institution to raise.

Institutions can also appoint internal monitoring and evaluation teams to work with change leaders and participants to establish benchmark measures, organize plans for data collection and analysis, offer regular opportunities for key leaders and participants to reflect on progress and identify areas for improvement, and contribute to messaging about the project. Examples of possible benchmark measures include the number of departments involved in efforts to change teaching evaluation, the stage of progress of each department involved, the campus activities related to the change process (e.g., workshops, conferences, celebrations), the number of people involved in the work, the policies that have been changed, the quality of change in promotion materials submitted, and the number of people offering portfolios with new approaches to presenting their work as teachers.

This kind of regular monitoring, tracking, assessing, and benchmarking of a change initiative is critical in achieving long-term institutionalization. Both monitoring (formative evaluation) and benchmarking of tangible progress (summative evaluation) are needed to advance a goal such as transforming teaching evaluation, which is deeply rooted in institutional practices, culture, and history. Those involved are well-served to consider this work a matter of continuous improvement, with more faculty and departments becoming engaged over time, strategies to engage in effective evaluation being adjusted through experimentation, and faculty commitment to meaningful student learning being expressed in conversations that enrich teaching practice.

Handling Resistance, Barriers, and Threats

While those working on a transformational change project may bring enthusiasm and commitment, the long-range impact and the possibility of deeply embedding the work into the culture and norms of the institution can be challenged by various barriers and threats. By definition, transformational change means that the way things have been done must change, and such a goal naturally means some resistance is likely to occur. Resistance may come from within or from outside the institution. Anticipating and preparing for resistance can improve the likelihood of institutional change.

Internal resistance may arise in relation to a change project related to teaching and learning, and specifically to teaching evaluation. Key leaders who support the change goal and provide resources and encouragement may depart or take on new roles, including provosts, vice provosts, deans, department chairs, or faculty leaders. A major source of resistance may come from people whose mental models about faculty work and teaching—and how it should be evaluated—are challenged by possible changes to an evaluation process they know. The social cognition theories mentioned earlier explain that when people experience cognitive dissonance as new ideas clash with ideas to which they are committed, they are likely to resist.[44] Transformative change, or second-order change, challenges values and norms and, thus, can create such dissonance; reluctance to participate or outright resistance may result. Resistance may also develop if faculty or administrative leaders perceive the intended change as out of alignment with institutional values and norms, as the cultural theories discussed earlier suggest.[45] For example, if institutional norms, priorities, and strategic plans, along with the faculty reward system, have historically elevated and emphasized research productivity, faculty members may have perceived that time spent on teaching-related work would not be highly valued. Thus, these faculty members might naturally be skeptical about calls for them to demonstrate their teaching perspectives and accomplishments more fully and devote time to new teaching evaluation processes. Institutional history may also generate resistance. For example, faculty members may be unenthusiastic about devoting time to new approaches to teaching evaluation if the institution has experienced unfunded and unsupported mandates for teaching-related change in the past.

Resistance to change may also have its roots external to the university or college. National or state agendas may focus attention on specific issues that require attention, such as when legislatures discuss higher education funding or when political groups raise questions or criticisms about curricular issues, campus activities, or leadership decisions within the academy. Such external pressures may divert institutional leaders' attention from important change projects and may thwart or diminish faculty interest in and motivation for investing their energies in new projects related to teaching. Unexpected societal events such as the pandemic, conflict in the broader world arena, or violence near the institution may also divert attention. Issues capturing attention across higher education, such as the rapid rise of generative artificial intelligence and its implications for higher education, may also make a change project less of a priority. Changes in the interests of external funding agencies, which can occur as societal issues gain attention or as the leadership in funding agencies shifts, can also undermine change efforts by removing available resources to support the work.

Managing resistance and barriers is part of fostering transformational change. Leaders of change efforts are wise to monitor and discuss with their colleagues the kinds of internal and external issues that may affect the change effort. Such monitoring will not affect the factors challenging the change work, but it can help change agents anticipate problems, prepare their colleagues for possible barriers, and enable planning for ways to address resistance. Resistance that emerges as people's mental models are challenged can be addressed through conversations with peers about what changes are needed and why they are important, the presentation of information about why and how the change is happening, and what supports are available. Reframing attention to teaching evaluation as part of a commitment to faculty excellence in teaching and research alike is one example of a change in mental models that leaders could encourage. As discussed earlier in the chapter, such conversations and information about what teaching means support the meaning-making that social cognition theories say is fruitful when people need to rethink their mental models and deal with cognitive dissonance.

Institutional leaders can be especially helpful in highlighting why the intended change is aligned with institutional values. Often, change leaders find it helpful to explicitly mention institutional strategic planning documents and how the change underway is aligned with and supports specific institutional priorities. If the change goal is not aligned with institutional priorities, senior-level leaders may need to explain any priority changes and how the change project will contribute to and align with those institutional shifts. Efforts to transform teaching evaluation may require specific attention to how these changes align with institutional policies, practices, and expectations around faculty evaluation overall. For example, faculty members being considered for promotion who present different forms of evidence about their teaching than is traditional might meet resistance from college-level and institution-level faculty review committees if those committees have not been briefed about the changes in teaching evaluation. Potential resistance from stakeholders across the institution (e.g., members of promotion committees, deans, students) can be diminished if they are regularly apprised of the discussions contributing to the change and the process of implementing new approaches to teaching evaluation. Furthermore, senior institutional leaders can make clear to faculty members and review committees at all levels of the institution that the efforts to update teaching evaluation seek to value more fully the (often hidden) work that faculty are already doing in their practice, and to ensure that evaluation happens "with," rather than "to," faculty members.

External events and issues are less easy to manage or change than those within a university or college. However, change leaders should stay abreast of key developments in the broader landscape so they can consider the implications for the institution and its change efforts. In some instances, institutional leaders may need to encourage change leaders to adjust their timelines or expectations as external pressures require attention. As they monitor the possible implications of external factors, institutional leaders can recognize that efforts to transform teaching evaluation might bolster institutional capacities to manage external factors by contributing to messaging about the value of higher education, the differences between faculty work and machine-based approaches, and the financial viability of high-quality teaching practices. Senior leaders can help their institutions walk the fine line between recognizing the implications of external matters that may slow change efforts while also ensuring that important internal aspirations, such as reforming teaching evaluation, are not forgotten or diminished in importance. Overall, managing resistance and barriers is one of the most important roles of senior leaders, which is addressed further in the suggestions for institutional leaders in chapter 4.

Connecting with External Partners

This chapter has focused primarily on how theories, frameworks, and principles help guide change leaders as they work within their institutions to foster transformative change. However, we also want to emphasize that a key factor in supporting and sustaining a transformative change initiative, such as improving teaching evaluation, is to link with external partners.

Research and examples point to the benefits that occur when individuals and groups work together. As mentioned earlier, the networked improvement model has been used in K–12 and higher education (particularly with community colleges) to connect organizations with common problems and goals, and to provide a structure through which they engage in continuous cycles of developing and applying interventions across different settings, testing and collecting data, and working together to learn and advance change.[46] The National Science Foundation has also used the principle of collective impact to encourage the creation of more equitable learning environments in higher education.[47] The power of cross-institutional collaboration and learning has also been built into the National Science Foundation's decades-long ADVANCE program, which has had much success in fostering more equitable workplaces in academe, particularly in STEM fields.[48]

The three universities we have studied have been part of the National Science Foundation-funded TEval project, which enabled change leaders at the three participating institutions to discuss and compare their use of the TEval approach and to learn together about strategies for advancing campus-level change in teaching evaluation. Our research has enabled us to observe and gather insights into the value of cross-institutional collaboration around significant change efforts. The project convened teams of department chairs, faculty members, and senior leaders from the three institutions through both in-person and Zoom-facilitated meetings. Enthusiasm for the opportunities to share ideas, strategies, and lessons has been high. Additionally, the TEval project convened several national meetings across the years of the project, sometimes in collaboration with the National Academies of Sciences' Roundtable on Systemic Change in Undergraduate STEM Education. Participants also reported great value from these opportunities to interact with peers at other institutions involved in similar work. The sense-making that we have discussed as critically important to fostering change is an important element and outcome of such meetings. Additionally, the involvement in a major change project along with peer institutions, and supported by a national agency, has provided much legitimacy to the work of institutions engaging in transformative change in teaching evaluation.

The research on interinstitutional collaboration and the benefits and outcomes experienced by the three case institutions indicate that connecting and partnering with other institutions is a useful lever to support institutions engaged in transforming teaching evaluation. More than fifty universities have also indicated interest in an emerging national alliance around reform in teaching evaluation. Thus, we anticipate new opportunities for productive, supportive, and inspiring cross-institutional learning and collaboration, especially because various funding agencies are contributing to a supportive external environment for transforming teaching evaluation.

IMPORTANT POINTS TO TAKE FROM THIS CHAPTER

To conclude this chapter, we highlight key ideas from research and practice on how transformative change occurs in higher education. In subsequent chapters, we translate these ideas into specific practical guidance, first for department leaders (chapter 3) and then for senior institutional leaders (chapter 4).

- *Take a systems approach and use theories of change*: Universities and colleges are complex organizations with many parts and different stakeholders. Reviewing theories that explain how change occurs and frameworks developed from research that highlight useful approaches to nurturing change, specifically in higher education, can provide good ideas. Adopting a single theory or a single framework is not necessary. Leaders can draw ideas from various theories and frameworks to help them create a plan that will fit with their institution.

- *Consider the particular institutional context*: Transforming teaching evaluation involves assessment of institutional readiness to engage in a change process, consideration of what change plans will fit the institutional context, and attention to the multiple levels of the organization. Examining the institutional culture and context, including institutional values, priorities, and history, helps leaders make decisions about what approaches to change are most likely to fit—and therefore, to be successful—within their specific context. Change plans also need to recognize that effective change efforts involve leaders at various organizational levels. That is, an integrated top-down, bottom-up, and middle-out approach involving senior institutional leaders, department-level leaders, and faculty members themselves will create a path toward a major goal, such as transforming teaching evaluation. This chapter has highlighted ways that institutional stakeholders in these different roles can make important contributions to the change process. This discussion about the important contributions of those in different institutional roles will continue in chapters 3 and 4.
- *Use multiple strategies*: Successful change efforts also depend on selecting and using multiple, synergistic strategies, or levers, for change that recognize the interrelated parts of a higher education institution. One way to design a set of complementary strategies is to consider the university or college and the overall goal to change teaching evaluation from different perspectives. For example, those committed to a change in teaching evaluation should consider strategies that address structural issues related to teaching evaluation, strategies that address the ability of people in the organization to

understand and do the work required to make the change, strategies that create a positive political context for the change, and symbolic strategies that help people make sense of the change in the context of organizational culture. Developing a comprehensive set of strategies to advance the change is a good way to optimize factors that encourage the change and minimize barriers.

- *Commit to sustaining change over time*: Sustaining change and planning for long-term success is not easy, especially in complex higher education organizations that have many projects underway in support of their overall missions. The literature emphasizes the importance of monitoring and evaluating a change process and setting benchmarks to assess progress over time. Changing teaching evaluation is a process of continuous improvement, where moving forward in steps and adjusting as needed is to be expected. Changing a university or college, especially in regard to its core work of teaching, takes time. Recognizing that the work will go through stages helps leaders see progress while also being mindful of challenges that arise. Modest steps, even seemingly small, if organized in the context of a systems approach, will add up to advance the larger goal.

The theories, frameworks, and principles explained in this chapter about change in complex organizations such as universities and colleges provide a foundation for the practical guidance offered in the next two chapters. In chapter 3, we explain how change in teaching evaluation needs to be understood in the context of departments, where faculty do so much of their work. Chapter 3 provides specific guidance to department leaders who seek to encourage their colleagues to envision and create new approaches to evaluate teaching. Then, in chapter 4, we speak to senior institutional leaders whose vision, support, and decisions are also central to a successful institutional plan to create holistic, equitable, and meaningful approaches to teaching evaluation.

3

Considerations for Department Leaders and Change Agents

THE TEVAL APPROACH IS based on the understanding that the department is the core unit of change for teaching evaluation. The department is where most faculty teach and is the primary unit for faculty evaluation and academic organization at most universities and colleges.[1] Although we center here on the academic department, we are confident this approach will also work at institutions where the college or division is the key unit of change (locus of primary evaluation), as is the case in some smaller institutions. Indeed, even within our institutions, there are some smaller schools or colleges (e.g., social welfare at the University of Kansas and computer science at the University of Massachusetts Amherst) that serve as a primary unit for academic organization. Thus, readers are encouraged to interpret the term *department* as appropriate to their context—the unit responsible for hiring, evaluating, promoting, and governing the faculty engaged in educational practices.

This chapter provides guidance to departments interested in changing their approach to teaching evaluation based on key principles of institutional change discussed in chapter 2, as well as our research involving more than eighty academic units across the University of Colorado Boulder (CU), the University of Kansas (KU), and the University of Massachusetts Amherst (UMass). The department-level change process encourages adaptation of a framework and associated tools, described in chapter 1, to support teaching evaluation approaches that are more equitable and transparent and that are more aligned with what is known about effective teaching than commonly used methods. As described earlier, the framework is organized around a rubric that articulates expectations for multiple dimensions of teaching contributions and draws on evidence from the instructor, students, and a peer or outside evaluator.[2] Our model for the department-level change process draws on the sense-making and organizational processes emphasized within social cognition change theories and models of continuous improvement.[3] The department-level change approach supports middle-out and bottom-up approaches to change while recognizing that leadership from the top (senior-level leaders) is also crucial to supporting successful and sustainable change within departments (see chapter 5).[4]

The remainder of this chapter is organized into four sections. First, we present scenarios from three departments in the TEval project to ground our discussion of change principles in real-world environments. These scenarios offer valuable insights into how departments navigate the complexities of the change process, adapting it to their unique circumstances, goals, and challenges. Next, we address how departments can prepare for the transformation process and the sorts of decisions they must make as they develop a plan to create more holistic approaches to teaching evaluation. For that, we return to the three cases and draw on other examples to illustrate how these preparatory steps play out in different department contexts. The third section describes the department-level change process, outlining the steps we recommend departments take to design, implement, refine, and sustain new approaches, again using exemplars from the TEval project to illustrate the variations and adaptations to consider. The final section provides cross-cutting lessons learned and recommendations for change leaders in addressing common barriers to department-level change.

THREE ILLUSTRATIVE DEPARTMENT SCENARIOS

In this section, we introduce examples from departments in the TEval project to illustrate the practical steps, timelines, challenges, and choices departments face as they change their approaches to teaching evaluation. These departmental examples, along with several additional department examples, are also available in fuller form on our project website, www.TEval.net. We will return to these scenarios later in the chapter to illustrate and explain the ways in which our recommendations interact with the affordances and limitations of different departmental and disciplinary contexts. Our goal is to provide a nuanced understanding of the change process, highlighting the diverse paths that departments can take in transforming teaching evaluation and offering practical lessons and strategic considerations for other departments embarking on similar change efforts.

Department Scenario 1: Transforming Teaching Evaluation for Promotion, Tenure, and Annual Review at the University of Colorado Boulder

Like many of the early adopter departments at CU, the Department of History had been involved in the university's decades-long efforts to transform undergraduate education and had a long-standing commitment to quality educational practices. Without consistent measures for teaching quality, though, faculty members found that the scholarly teaching practices they adopted were not reflected in the evaluation process. The department thus sought to elevate scholarly teaching in its reward system and transform it from an individual pursuit to a shared departmental commitment. The Department of History used the TEval approach and tools to revamp its processes for high-stakes, summative teaching evaluation, including promotion, tenure, and annual review. They also sought to better align with and reward the student-centered and scholarly teaching practices that previous work had advanced. As one of the early opt-in departments in CU's TEval work (i.e., the Teaching Quality Framework initiative), the history department formed a working group to address teaching evaluation. A couple of years into the process, the history department's work fulfilled a charge by the dean for departments to develop externalized measures of teaching quality. Before TEval, the department had used an internal grant to develop program learning objectives across courses.[5] They built on these learning objectives for the teaching evaluation effort, using tools and rubrics modified from other campus approaches (e.g., KU's Benchmarks framework) to develop a suite of new practices, resources, and policies around teaching evaluation. Those included an externalized definition of teaching effectiveness, a peer review process consisting of observation and pre- and post-observation conversations, and guidance for self-reflection. Team members participated in and contributed to campus-wide dialogues and meetings around teaching quality and also took part in national meetings of the TEval network. The department ran a one-year pilot of the processes developed by the working group, followed by a survey to gather feedback about department members' satisfaction with the new system. The survey revealed very positive responses. The full faculty approved the processes, which are currently used for promotion, tenure, and annual review. The Department of History's work on teaching evaluation also contributed to their preparation for accreditation review and their meeting of related accreditation standards.

Department Scenario 2: From Formative Peer Review to Full-Scale Transformation of Teaching Evaluation at the University of Kansas

The Department of Chemical and Petroleum Engineering at the University of Kansas joined the TEval project to foster more authentic and effective implementation of KU's evaluation policy, which requires examining multiple dimensions of teaching through multiple lenses: instructor, peer, and students. The department particularly wanted to enhance its processes for gathering information from peers, recognizing the potential of peer review as a formative tool for mentoring and teaching improvement. Whereas the CU Department of History (scenario 1) focused from the beginning on reforming summative evaluation practices, KU's Department of Chemical and Petroleum Engineering made its entry point into transforming teaching evaluation the launch of peer review triads to support teaching development among early-career faculty.

At the outset of the initiative, the department had a large cohort of pretenure faculty members. Leaders of the department initiative saw the TEval project as an opportunity to bolster an existing mentoring committee's support for the teaching success of junior faculty. Two department team members had previously worked with the KU Center for Teaching Excellence to design and lead a peer triad program, which arranged cross-department faculty triads for formative peer review and pedagogical development. The department team adapted this approach using the TEval framework and tools to support peer review activities among peer triads and quads. Initially, the effort involved members of the mentoring committee who volunteered to test the new approaches while building broader interest. Team members participated in and contributed to a cross-department community around the reform of teaching evaluation and also took part in national meetings of the TEval network. After three years, the department voted to implement a suite of new practices and resources for all teaching evaluation processes—both formative and summative—that are based on TEval approaches. Three events precipitated the department vote. The first was a change in department leadership; a faculty member who had long-standing involvement in teaching innovation and who was on the department project team became department chair. Second, moving the university-wide student survey of teaching online led to significantly reduced response rates and prompted department members to seek information about alternative measures of teaching effectiveness. Third, the department applied for one of five $100,000 awards from the Association of American Universities' Undergraduate STEM Initiative to support the development and implementation of innovative department models for teaching evaluation, and they were successful in securing that award. All faculty now participate in peer review triads or quads, organized by course sequences, and the Benchmarks rubric and documentation from three lenses (students, peers, and the instructor) are used for teaching evaluation in promotion, tenure, and annual review.

Department Scenario 3: Peer Review to Advance Pedagogical Development at the University of Massachusetts Amherst

As described earlier, the University of Massachusetts Amherst effort was largely motivated by widespread faculty frustration with traditional student evaluations. That frustration became acute when the institution created innovative classroom spaces to foster collaborative and active learning, and students responded (initially) negatively to the new methods. The Department of Linguistics was one of several departments that had become dissatisfied with the reliance on student surveys in teaching evaluation and was interested in shifting to more holistic approaches. The department has a strong teaching culture with a deep commitment to high-quality teaching. They developed and implemented an educational effectiveness plan (EEP) that specified learning objectives across the curriculum, and the department chair saw this as well-aligned with the goals of TEval. Seeing this natural alignment, the department used the elements of the TEval framework to foster conversation around teaching and to support the implementation of its educational effectiveness program. The department chair and three tenured faculty members led the initiative to implement more holistic evaluation methods, beginning with peer midterm assessments for mentoring and self-evaluation. The team used the TEval approach to guide the formation and activities of two triads that were structured around course similarity and faculty interests. One triad was focused on the use of peer review to improve course outcomes within an introductory course. The second applied peer observation in a round-robin fashion to share best practices and encourage discussions of teaching. The project has garnered significant interest in the department in continuing these positive triad experiences and expanding the evidence used. In fall 2022, the triad approach was tabled in the department due to staffing, time, and other university mandates that required immediate attention. Nevertheless, the department found significant benefit overall because faculty members are now more knowledgeable about the ways to evaluate teaching beyond the student survey. The department continues to use TEval resources, such as the rubric, to guide the mentoring process.

PREPARING FOR CHANGE

To get started, departments seeking to engage in the transformation of their approach to teaching evaluation need to assess and reflect on their department context and readiness for change, identify the purpose, audience, and parameters of their change effort, and cultivate interest and develop a team to lead the effort. We describe each of these considerations in the sections that follow and then illustrate how they have played out in specific department cases in the TEval project.

Examine Departmental Context and Assess Readiness

The change literature reviewed in chapter 2 suggests that the initiation of a transformational change initiative should begin with an assessment of the department context with particular attention to department readiness for change in approaches to teaching evaluation. This crucial step sets the stage for effective planning and implementation. We recommend that the assessment center on three key questions to gauge the department's current state and determine the best path forward.

What Foundation Exists for This Effort?

First, department leaders should assess the current status of teaching evaluation in the department and the degree of departmental awareness of the need for change. By taking stock of the department's current approaches to teaching evaluation, the strengths and weaknesses of those approaches, and any history of efforts to improve teaching review and evaluation, the department can pinpoint needs and goals for transforming teaching evaluation along with opportunities to build on current and past work. For instance, at the outset of the TEval project, the Physics Department at UMass had a personnel subcommittee that was tasked with coming up with new methods for evaluation beyond student surveys; thus, the TEval initiative provided a structure for considering different sources of evidence. Additionally, department leaders should gauge faculty members' knowledge and mindsets about this work, including the department's current commitment to effective and inclusive teaching, the degree to which department members are cognizant of the limitations of current approaches, and their awareness of and interest in newer approaches to evaluation. This assessment can help department leaders understand the scope of work needed to promote widespread interest and uptake of new approaches and identify possible team members and champions for the effort.

What Is Motivating the Department to Do This Work Now?

Identifying and understanding the motivations for change is another important component of a departmental needs and readiness assessment. In some cases, the effort may be a response to external pressures or encouragement, such as new institutional mandates, policy changes, shifts in strategic priorities, or evolving disciplinary expectations. For example, at KU, several departments explored multisource approaches to teaching evaluation in response to the temporary suspension of student surveys of teaching during the COVID-19 pandemic. Such external catalysts can provide a powerful impetus for departments to reevaluate their practices. Motivation may also stem from internal drivers that arise from the department itself. These may include faculty dissatisfaction with current evaluation processes or structural changes that necessitate new approaches, such as the introduction of teaching faculty or the arrival of a large cohort of early-career faculty. The TEval project revealed a diverse array of internal motivations among the more than eighty participating academic units, such as minimizing bias in teaching evaluation, better documenting of faculty contributions to teaching innovation and student success, recognizing and rewarding faculty in new teaching stream roles, and improving mentoring for new faculty through transparent expectations.

Importantly, departments often enter into this work with multiple, overlapping motivations. Understanding this complex landscape of motivations allows department leaders to frame the work in ways that resonate with their colleagues. By connecting teaching evaluation reform to broader departmental goals—such as enhancing overall teaching quality, supporting new faculty, or advancing equity in faculty assessment—leaders can generate broader buy-in and momentum for change. This strategic alignment of motivations with departmental objectives is crucial to fostering a collective commitment to transforming teaching evaluation practices.

What Is the Department's Culture and Overall Health?

A third set of considerations in a department's readiness for teaching evaluation reform is its culture around decision-making, collaborative work, and overall health. First, departments should reflect on their history of collaboration and shared decision-making, particularly in relation to teaching and learning, sense of shared responsibility for student learning, the role of departmental leadership in encouraging collaboration and improvement, and the degree to which faculty feel empowered to contribute to departmental decisions and initiatives, all of which contribute to the department's teaching culture and readiness for change.[6] Within the TEval initiative, we observed that departments with robust cultures of teaching and learning were often better prepared to tackle full-scale reform of teaching evaluation than those with less history of collaboration or shared commitment to teaching innovation. Additionally, the disciplinary context, including norms and expectations regarding teaching and its evaluation, can inform, constrain, or enhance efforts to change teaching evaluation. Finally, department leaders must consider internal and external pressures facing the department, both current and anticipated. Those pressures can significantly shape the approach to and feasibility of reform. For instance, departments strained by low faculty numbers or significant budget reductions may not have the bandwidth to undertake a new change effort unless the reform can help them directly address these challenges.

Department self-assessment of the groundwork, motivations, and department culture and health can help leaders and change agents realistically evaluate their readiness for change. The literature on institutional change and our work within the TEval project suggest that the degree of departmental readiness for change in teaching evaluation can be gauged by awareness of a need for improved evaluation, interest and motivation to change among faculty, commitment from department leadership, bandwidth and resources for enacting change, and a department culture that supports teaching excellence and collaborative decision-making.[7] The self-assessment process can also help departments ascertain the optimal objectives and starting points for the work, identify key change strategies and levers, anticipate potential sources of friction, and assemble a team to lead the effort, all of which are important components of the initiation of meaningful teaching evaluation reform. We elaborate on these issues in the next sections.

Develop Transformation Objectives

Identify Evaluation Purpose or Context

Before beginning the change initiative, department leaders will need to select the evaluation purpose or context around which to focus their efforts. As outlined in chapter 1, the TEval model is designed to support holistic evaluation processes that integrate information from multiple lenses and provide a unifying framework for different evaluation processes. Nonetheless, there may be particular sources of evidence or evaluation processes that most need reshaping or that could serve as a starting point for the work, with the goal of transforming and aligning all processes in subsequent phases of work. For instance, some departments may aim to improve one or more of their systems for formal, summative evaluation, such as promotion and tenure or annual review. Others may focus on formative, growth-oriented evaluation, such as mentoring of early career faculty or the formation of peer review dyads or triads to foster intellectual exchange and improvement of student learning. Still others may wish to focus on developing or refining the collection and curation of evidence from a particular lens. Our work with departments in the TEval initiative demonstrates that each of these options has different affordances and limitations that interact with the change process. In table 3.1 we summarize examples of evaluation contexts or processes to which a TEval-based approach could be applied.

Our department-level change model emphasizes iteration and continuous improvement; thus, some departments may find it useful to identify short-term objectives as well as longer-term objectives that the department's work will build toward in an incremental way. The choice of where to begin teaching evaluation reform should be informed by what is learned through the department needs and readiness assessment, including opportunities to build on past work, processes the department is happy with, motivations for the change effort, and the level of department readiness. While full-scale transformation of "high-stakes"

TABLE 3.1 Evaluation purposes that could be transformed through multidimensional and multisource methods

Evaluation purpose	*Possible changes*
Teaching evaluation for promotion and tenure or reappointment	• Develop more robust processes for documenting and evaluating teaching for promotion and tenure decisions. • Examine multiple types of teaching contributions and draw on multiple lenses or sources of evidence. • Develop guidelines for candidate teaching dossiers and shared, transparent criteria to assess teaching development.
Teaching evaluation for annual review	• Transform processes for documenting and evaluating teaching in annual review. • Develop a multidimensional, multisource, and transparent process that can be feasibly carried out annually. • Design a template for annual documentation of teaching. • Develop a process for evaluating that evidence in annual review.
Teaching statements or self-reflection	• Develop a process and guidance for instructors to develop reflective narratives for annual, promotion, or tenure review. • Help instructors go beyond statements of teaching philosophy to document the intellectual work involved in effective teaching and facilitating learning, as well as the care that goes into creating a motivating and inclusive learning climate.
Building dossiers of materials or teaching portfolios	• Develop guidance for the development of robust and coherent supporting materials or course portfolios that illustrate an instructor's approaches to teaching and the impact on student learning and the student experience. • Often paired with guidance for the reflective narrative, which can serve as a guide to the supplemental documentation.
Peer or "third-party" review	• Develop or improve the collection of evidence from a peer or third-party lens. • Initiate a peer review process or redesign an existing process to be more systematic and consistent and to capture the intellectual work involved in effective teaching. • Develop a process for using third-party observation tools to document the frequency with which evidence-based teaching practices are used in the classroom.[8]
Collection and use of student feedback	• Improve the student rating tool itself. • Develop a process to support instructor reflection on and use of student feedback. • Explore tools for gathering additional forms of student feedback (e.g., surveys about mentorship).

teaching evaluation (e.g., promotion, tenure, reappointment, and annual review) is the ultimate goal of initiatives like TEval, it may not be the optimal starting point for all departments. Departments that successfully transformed high-stakes evaluation processes in the TEval project typically demonstrated a high degree of readiness, characterized by strong motivations for change (responding to internal or external drivers), a robust teaching culture with a history of collaborative decision-making, broad faculty awareness of and interest in improved evaluation approaches, support from department leadership, and bandwidth and resources for enacting change, along with opportunities to build on existing initiatives.

For departments at lower levels of readiness or those whose motivations were more centered on teaching development, a focus on improving information collection from a particular lens (e.g., self-reflection or peer review) often proved to be an effective starting point. The choice among these options may also be influenced by alignment with other department goals related to teaching and learning. For instance, a focus on peer review or the use of third-party observation tools might be particularly appealing to departments that want to develop formative evaluation processes that support instructors' pedagogical improvement or foster greater dialogue about teaching and learning. Departments aiming to promote more reflective teaching and assessment of student learning might begin by focusing on self-reflection and teaching portfolios. Departments might choose to begin their work in one evaluation context and move into the transformation of other processes over time. Indeed, several departments that were involved with the TEval project initially focused on establishing formative peer review processes, later expanding their approach to include promotion, tenure, and annual reviews.

Identify the Audience

Departments also need to decide for whom they wish to change the evaluation process. In other words, which subset(s) of instructors (e.g., pretenure faculty, teaching stream faculty) will be involved at the start of the project to change teaching evaluation? Possible groups to involve include pretenure faculty, posttenure faculty, teaching assistants, VITAL faculty (visiting, instructors, temporary, adjunct, and lecturers), or some subset of them.[9] Even if a department chooses to focus on one instructor subset, we recommend that definitions of teaching effectiveness and development be aligned across instructor groups; the expectations for achievement of different levels of teaching development might vary for instructors in different career phases.

Selecting a target audience for teaching evaluation reform, much like choosing the focal evaluation context, should be guided by the department's needs and readiness assessment. Additionally, departments might choose to begin their efforts with one group of instructors with a longer-term goal of scaling to a broader group. The TEval initiative highlighted various departmental approaches to audience selection, each tailored to specific departmental contexts and goals. Some departments found that VITAL faculty were more receptive to robust teaching evaluation approaches, as teaching is their primary responsibility, and these new approaches recognized the full scope of their contributions. Other departments focused on early-career faculty or graduate teaching assistants, who tended to be more open to innovative methods. These approaches also helped them understand department expectations around teaching, thereby enhancing their pedagogical development. Departments that enjoyed broad faculty support or that had change initiatives targeting more modest shifts in practice (e.g., using the rubric or a protocol to bring consistency to an existing peer review process) often applied new approaches to all instructors, ensuring equity and consistency in defining and rewarding excellent teaching. Conversely, some departments opted to pilot new methods with a subset of the intended audience to demonstrate the value of the approaches and encourage wider acceptance. For example, faculty members nearing promotion might agree to pilot new methods, or departments could start with a "coalition of the willing" before scaling to the rest of the faculty. This strategic audience selection not only facilitates the initial implementation but also lays a foundation for the broader adoption of reformed teaching evaluation practices across the department.

Identify Potential Facilitating Factors and Barriers

Another important step in preparing for teaching evaluation reform is the identification of potential facilitating factors that can increase the likelihood of successful change. Identifying and leveraging resources, models, and allies before the launch of a department change effort can help shape the focus of the transformation and the plan and strategies that are enacted and can facilitate the recruitment of a team to carry it out. It will be similarly critical for department initiative leaders to anticipate at the outset where resistance might come from to manage barriers that could impede department-level teaching reform with proactive strategies. Like the identification of enabling factors, proactive barrier identification enables departments to integrate targeted strategies into their project plan, such as building broad coalitions of support, creating robust succession plans, establishing clear timelines that account for competing demands, and designing interventions to address cultural resistance, before launching their reform efforts. Bolman and Deal's four frames, as discussed in chapter 2, provide a useful framework for departments to scan for potential enablers and barriers of change both within and outside of the department.[10]

The Structural Frame

Through the structural frame, departments could inventory existing assets: current policies and practices that align with the desired changes; department committees (e.g., mentoring or evaluation committees) that could provide structural support; institutional resources (e.g., teaching and learning centers) that could offer expertise and infrastructure; existing tools and resources for collecting documentation of teaching effectiveness from different sources; and models from other departments whose experiences could inform their approaches. In the TEval project, all departments had access to tools and resources developed by the project team, such as the rubrics, peer review and observation protocols, and self-reflection templates described in chapter 1, that could be used as starting points and scaffolding for the department's work. Additionally, many departments in the TEval project strategically aligned their work to improve teaching evaluation with pre-existing departmental structures, including educational effectiveness plans, peer review requirements, and mentoring committees to support early-career faculty.

Conversely, the structural frame can also help departments evaluate barriers that could hinder implementation. These include gaps in existing infrastructure, such as inadequate data systems, assessment processes, or administrative support. Departments should also scan their upcoming commitments—such as planned accreditation visits, program reviews, or curriculum revisions—that could compete for attention and resources (or that could be used to leverage interest in changes to teaching evaluation, as was done by the CU History Department as they prepared for an accreditation review). TEval departments with successful initiative launches typically addressed these barriers by either aligning their change efforts to support other commitments or deferring an active change effort until other commitments were wrapped up.

By considering both facilitating factors and barriers through the structural frame, departments can leverage existing strengths while proactively addressing potential obstacles, thereby creating a more conducive environment for change.

The Human Resources Frame

The human resources frame emphasizes the importance of identifying change agents and champions who will lead departmental efforts as well as how their work will be supported. In the TEval project, this involved recruiting faculty members into the effort who had demonstrated commitment to teaching excellence and openness to innovation and offering support mechanisms, such as stipends, course releases, and professional development opportunities, to protect the team members' time and provide the recognition and support that was needed to recruit them and sustain their engagement. For instance, both KU and UMass provided departmental grants to support teams' work on behalf of their departments, whereas CU provided departments with substantial support from postdoctoral fellows. Existing communities of transformation within and outside the institution, such as the multi-institutional network that formed around the TEval project, can also provide valuable support and opportunities for sense-making and sense-giving.

Also, through the human resources lens, departments need to gauge faculty capacity and readiness for change, considering current workloads, potential retirements or departures, and the stability of leadership positions that would be crucial for sustained reform. This includes assessing whether key champions have secure positions and sufficient bandwidth to guide the initiative. In the TEval project, several department efforts ultimately stalled after the departure of key team members or changes in department leadership; thus, departments will want to establish robust teams with shared leadership and a succession plan so that the effort is well-positioned to weather such transitions (more on assembling a team below).

The Political Frame

The political frame directs attention to identifying potential allies who have power in and influence on the change effort. In TEval, many departments' efforts were advanced by the involvement of one or more highly respected department members at the launch of the project. Additionally, TEval departments benefitted from having allies in university administration, faculty governance, and the broader higher education community.

Many of these coalitions were initiated and nurtured by the individuals or central unit leading the campus-level initiative. As described in chapters 2 and 4, before the launch of the project, TEval leaders on each campus secured commitments and partnerships with university- and school-level leadership to help align unit or institutional expectations with TEval-based approaches. They also created campus-wide communities or stakeholder groups to generate interest and broaden awareness of new approaches. For instance, in response to a pause in the use of the student survey of teaching at KU during the COVID-19 pandemic, the Center for Teaching Excellence created a department chairs working group to explore alternative mechanisms for teaching evaluation. The group included several chairs of departments that were early adopters of the TEval framework. At the conclusion of the working group, almost all of the chairs brought their departments into the Benchmarks initiative. CU built on the national AAU Undergraduate STEM Education Initiative, and a small coalition of department chairs was instrumental in securing support from university leadership before the launch of the TEval project for the effort to transform teaching evaluation. After several meetings, the coalition members approached the provost and sought recognition of the proposed work and confirmation that it aligned with the campus strategies for advancing the institution's student success priorities. With the provost's approval and support, the initiative launched. Understanding institutional political dynamics and developing allies among relevant stakeholders can help departments build necessary coalitions, navigate organizational barriers, and secure necessary approvals once the work begins. Similar early engagement with the provost at UMass took place before the formal start of the TEval project to discuss the concept and its goals. The meeting included the leaders of the faculty union, an important ally at a campus with strong union representation. The provost, the union, and the project leaders were able to reach an agreement on the approach and parameters for TEval that would align with and support their mutual goals.

The political frame also prompts examination of departmental power dynamics and potential sources of resistance, such as influential faculty members who might oppose changes to evaluation practices or competing priorities that might emerge in resource allocation decisions. These sorts of political barriers emerged in several TEval departments whose early efforts involved coalitions of the willing (e.g., junior faculty, lecturers, or graduate teaching assistants who were more open to new approaches), but who did not themselves feel empowered to advance widespread reform. For instance, multiple departments on the three campuses had their work stalled when senior faculty objected to changes to the evaluation process, and, in response, some of these departments limited their TEval focus to new faculty, teaching-stream faculty, or graduate teaching assistants. In other instances, senior faculty cited a history of distrust with campus-level and administrative initiatives that were communicated as voluntary or faculty-led but turned out to be permanent or lacked sufficient faculty input. As another example, concerns about overwork during the COVID-19 pandemic led a cluster of faculty at UMass to persuade their department to pause involvement in the TEval project. These potential sources of friction necessitate the adoption of strategic plans to broaden engagement. Plans might situate the initial effort as a proof-of-concept, include substantial participant voice, and enact early social and symbolic interventions, such as engaging with the national dialogue, external communities, or campus-wide stakeholder groups before soliciting departmental teams.

The Symbolic Frame

Finally, the symbolic frame suggests developing an internal vision or narrative around the change goal and identifying cultural assets and communities that can reinforce the initiative's value and bring legitimacy to the work. Cultural assets and communities might include disciplinary and departmental norms, university mission and priorities, disciplinary societies, and multi-institutional networks and higher education organizations that offer symbolic messages about the value of more holistic, valid, and equitable teaching evaluation. These symbolic levers could be used in the preparatory phase to inform the objectives of the effort and cultivate interest in the work. For instance, the School of Social Welfare at the University of Kansas framed its initiative as an opportunity to align reward and recognition processes with the field of social work's disciplinary values, which center the advancement of equity and inclusion. Departments in the TEval project also found inspiration in the AAU Undergraduate STEM Education Initiative and the National Academies' Roundtable on Systemic Change in Undergraduate Education, both of which have helped stimulate a national dialogue around the need to align teaching evaluation with what is known about effective educational practices.[11]

The symbolic frame can also bring attention to cultural barriers within or outside the department, such as deeply held beliefs about teaching and teaching evaluation that are challenged by new methods, historical resistance to change, or potential conflicts with departmental identity and values. In TEval, department and initiative leaders used levers from the symbolic frame to highlight the value of the work and address cultural resistance. Early identification of these assets and barriers can help the department shape the focus of the transformation and develop a narrative that will resonate with department members, recruit team members, and position the planned reforms within broader movements for educational enhancement before the work begins.

Cultivate Interest and Assemble a Team

To cultivate interest in the change initiative, department leaders should build upon insights gained from the department's readiness assessment, tailoring their approach to the existing level of awareness of new approaches and motivation for change within the department. To identify effective entry points for engaging colleagues and to craft a narrative that resonates with faculty while aligning with departmental culture, change leaders should consider the facilitating factors discussed earlier. Effective strategies could include the following:

- Emphasizing how changes can benefit faculty members by bringing recognition to teaching contributions typically overlooked or undervalued by current evaluation methods
- Providing resources and support for those who agree to take the lead on the work
- Highlighting how the change effort could address specific department needs or align with departmental values, disciplinary norms, or broader institutional priorities
- Engaging respected faculty members as early advocates to lend credibility to the effort
- Leveraging external organizations, networks, and institutions to normalize new approaches and underscore the value of the work
- Drawing attention to national dialogues on teaching excellence and equitable evaluation practices, thereby legitimizing the reform effort and positioning it as part of a larger movement in higher education

Throughout this process, it is important to proactively address potential concerns and emphasize how the changes can benefit both individual faculty members and the department as a whole.

Once sufficient interest and resources have been confirmed, department leaders should assemble a departmental team to transform a department's teaching evaluation process. Approaches to team construction will depend on the department's readiness, including who has been involved in early groundwork, familiarity with new approaches, motivation for the initiative, and the culture surrounding collaboration. Ideally, the team should encompass a mix of full professors, early-career faculty, and VITAL faculty to ensure diverse perspectives, with explicit backing from the department chair. Recruitment methods can vary. Leaders might leverage existing committees, issue department-wide calls for volunteers, assign specific roles, or target individuals for recruitment.

It is advantageous to include members who have served on personnel committees (such as merit or promotion and tenure committees) or who are engaged in faculty mentoring. To support this effort, departments should establish clear goals and expectations, create a regular meeting schedule, and secure commitments from participants. Importantly, team members should be incentivized through mechanisms like teaching, service credit, or summer stipends. This approach not only enhances immediate functionality but also ensures long-term sustainability, even amid leadership transitions and changes in team membership.

DEPARTMENT SCENARIOS: ILLUSTRATING DIVERSE PATHWAYS TO INITIATE CHANGE EFFORTS

We now return to the three department scenarios presented at the beginning of this chapter, using them to provide more holistic illustrations of how these principles of preparing for change manifest and interact in specific departmental contexts. By revisiting these scenarios through the lens of our framework for preparing for change, we can see how departments navigate the complexities of initiating teaching evaluation reform within their unique contexts.

Scenario 1: History at CU

The Department of History at CU had a high level of readiness before initiating change in its teaching evaluation processes. They built upon a strong foundation of commitment to high-quality education and previous work on program learning objectives. This existing groundwork provided a solid starting point for reform efforts. Their motivation initially stemmed from internal drivers (a desire for consistent measures of teaching quality), although it later aligned with external motivating factors (a charge from the dean to develop externalized measures). The department's culture of shared responsibility for student learning and collaborative decision-making facilitated the formation of a working group to lead the initiative on behalf of the entire department. The department's high level of readiness and motivation to develop a more consistent and collaborative approach to documenting teaching quality positioned initiative leaders to focus on high-stakes summative evaluation processes from the beginning of their effort. The department chair also saw that efforts to prepare for an accreditation visit could be leveraged to encourage involvement in changing teaching evaluation—and vice versa. Both efforts required faculty to look closely at the department's intended learning outcomes.

Scenario 2: Chemical and Petroleum Engineering at KU

The Department of Chemical and Petroleum Engineering at KU began its work at a lower level of readiness to work on high-stakes evaluation processes than the first department case. A handful of faculty were aware of alternative approaches to evaluating teaching and were interested in exploring those approaches. Those interested faculty members designed the initial phases of their project to intentionally build interest and capacity for broader change. They created a coalition of the willing through an existing mentoring committee that was committed to supporting the development of teaching and the success of a large cohort of junior faculty members. They also had an opportunity to build on two senior faculty members' experiences designing and leading cross-department peer-review triads. With these issues in mind, they launched their initiative with a focus on formative peer review for early career faculty. This approach allowed them to address a specific departmental need (mentoring early-career faculty) and leverage some departmental assets (prior experience with formative peer review triads) while building broader interest in teaching evaluation reform.

Scenario 3: Linguistics at UMass

The Linguistics Department at UMass illustrates how a department can leverage an initiative to improve teaching evaluation in ways that build upon existing strengths and address specific needs and objectives. Rather than aiming for a comprehensive overhaul of high-stakes evaluation processes, the Linguistics Department joined the TEval project to enhance its formative evaluation practices and foster peer dialogue about teaching practices. The department's strong teaching culture and previously developed educational effectiveness plan provided a solid foundation for this work. By focusing on midterm assessments for mentoring and self-evaluation, implemented in faculty triads or dyads, faculty members aligned their efforts with their goal of fostering pedagogical development and collegial exchange around teaching.

THE DEPARTMENT CHANGE PROCESS

Once departments have moved through the preparatory steps of assessing their context, identifying project objectives, and assembling a team, they can turn their focus to the process of change. In this section, we present a model for department-level transformation that draws on insights from the organizational change literature and our observations of departments in the TEval initiative. Our model is grounded in theories of sense-making, sense-giving, organizational learning, and continuous improvement, each of which was discussed in chapter 2.[12] These theoretical frameworks provide a robust foundation for understanding processes through which departments can accomplish transformational change. Sense-making involves collaborative processes through which department members collectively develop a shared understanding of the change goal and process, often leading to new perspectives and insights along the way. Sense-giving involves effectively communicating the change goal to others so that it resonates and becomes meaningful to them. Organizational learning, which is often paired with sense-making, is the process by which an organization uses data and new knowledge to make collective, evidence-informed decisions for improvement. Continuous improvement models emphasize the value of iterative learning cycles, often referred to as "plan-do-study-act" cycles, that involve planning a change, enacting it, assessing the results, and making improvements based on those outcomes.[13]

Reflecting these principles, our model for department-level transformation involves iterative cycles of the following processes:

1) Defining effective teaching and building consensus around that definition
2) Identifying forms of evidence that can document and represent an instructor's practices on the defined elements
3) Developing a system for collecting and using the evidence for the intended evaluation contexts
4) Implementing the system and monitoring the results
5) Using the results to refine approaches and (if needed) expand the scale and scope of the change effort

In the next section, we explore each of these steps in-depth, examining how they can lead academic departments toward teaching evaluation reform and provide a practical roadmap for departments embarking on their own transformation initiative. We will also use our examples from departments across the three TEval universities to highlight how these steps interact and play out holistically within different department contexts to offer additional insights for navigating the complex process of departmental change.

Defining Teaching Effectiveness

The externalization of a shared definition of teaching effectiveness is a cornerstone of the framework for change that we have developed through the TEval project. Regardless of the evaluation context and specific focal purposes of department-level work on teaching evaluation, this process needs to be anchored in a common externalization or definition of teaching effectiveness. The rationale for this assertion is twofold. From a change theory perspective, a collaborative process of defining teaching effectiveness fosters a common vision among department members. Establishing a common vision aligns with key change strategies highlighted in multiple theoretical frameworks, including Henderson et al.'s four-quadrant taxonomy of change approaches and the symbolic frame of Bolman and Deal's model.[14] The act of cocreating or adapting a definition serves as a powerful tool for building consensus and shared understanding, essential elements for successful organizational change.

From a practical standpoint, a common definition of teaching effectiveness significantly enhances the evaluation process. It promotes greater transparency by clearly articulating expectations, ensures consistency in assessment across different evaluators and contexts, and contributes to fairness by establishing a uniform standard against which all faculty members are evaluated. This shared understanding creates a solid foundation for meaningful and sustainable change in evaluation practices, improving both the quality and equity of the resulting system.

However, reaching a consensus definition of teaching effectiveness can be a time- and labor-intensive process, particularly among faculty with diverse perspectives, experiences, and implicit assumptions about teaching, and who may lack a common language to discuss pedagogy. To address this challenge, department teams often benefit from using external frameworks that identify elements of good teaching, such as the rubric-based frameworks described in chapter 2, as a starting point. We recommend that teams approach this as a process of adapting the framework to their specific departmental and disciplinary context while also considering any existing institutional and school standards. Team members can also reflect on how they allocate their time in teaching to ensure all relevant elements are represented in their definition. For example, the Department of Germanic and Slavic Languages and Literatures at CU modified the rubric in CU's Teaching Quality Framework using elements of Bloom's taxonomy, elevating components that best aligned with their teaching efforts. Similarly, the School of Social Welfare at KU created an adaptation of KU's Benchmarks for Teaching Effectiveness rubric to center social justice and the advancement of diversity, equity, and inclusion, which are central to the disciplinary culture of social work.

While the process of building consensus around the department's definition of teaching effectiveness may initially begin with the project team, ideally, it should be presented to the full department for discussion and approval. This broader engagement is needed for widespread buy-in and to provide opportunities for all department members to become aware of and contribute to the standards so that it truly represents a shared vision. Indeed, this step offers the department a valuable opportunity to articulate its values around teaching and supporting learning, creating a solid foundation for both teaching and teaching evaluation efforts.

To summarize, key recommendations for the process of defining teaching effectiveness include the following:

1) Using an existing framework as a starting point
2) Adapting the framework to the department context and institutional standards and priorities
3) Involving the full department in building consensus around the definition
4) Avoiding overly prescriptive approaches by articulating a generalized enough set of criteria for the dimensions of effective teaching to accommodate different teaching contexts (e.g., online teaching, laboratory teaching) and styles
5) Planning for review and revision as teaching practices and priorities evolve over time

Identifying Forms of Evidence

After defining the elements of effective teaching, departments need to map these definitions onto evidence and artifacts that can effectively document an instructor's contributions in each domain. Although we present this as a second step, some departments in the TEval initiative found it beneficial to review various tools for collecting evidence (e.g., observation tools, faculty survey instruments) concurrently with defining effective teaching. This parallel process can help departments articulate a more comprehensive and practical definition of effective teaching.

For departments undertaking a comprehensive overhaul of their evaluation processes, this evidence mapping should consider sources of evidence drawn from each of the three lenses (self, student, and peer/third-party) and aligned with each dimension of teaching effectiveness. Departments focusing on improving the evaluation process for a particular lens need to consider the sorts of materials that will document the elements of good teaching from that source. The frameworks described in chapter 1 provide valuable guidance for this step of the process, as they include tools that link each dimension of teaching to specific types of materials from each source that can document teaching quality. Numerous additional resources and tools for this process are also available on our project website, www.TEval.net. When deciding what evidence to collect and review, departments should balance comprehensiveness with feasibility. The goal is to provide a holistic view of teaching effectiveness while ensuring that the process of collecting and reviewing evidence is manageable and sustainable. It is important to note that the same piece of evidence can often address multiple dimensions of teaching effectiveness. For instance, a well-designed syllabus might demonstrate both the clarity of course learning objectives and the community standards that an instructor uses to create a respectful and open class climate. Leveraging such multipurpose materials can help streamline the evaluation process. It will also be important for departments to consider ways to package and connect different artifacts and evidence for use in evaluation processes. For instance, evaluation committees may find themselves at a loss with what to look for in a dossier of assorted course materials unless those supplemental documents are framed by a short narrative that provides a guide to the supporting evidence.

Developing Processes for Use

Before implementing new approaches to teaching evaluation using new definitions, evidence, and tools, department teams will need to make decisions about what the implementation of a new system will look like. This requires consideration of timelines, roles, and products, and decisions will likely vary based on the department's goals and context. With regard to timelines and frequency, departments must determine when and how often different types of evidence, such as peer reviews or faculty statements about their teaching and students' learning, will be collected. They will also need to determine the appropriate scope (i.e., breadth and depth) of the documentation with respect to the instructor's teaching responsibilities (i.e., number of types of courses taught) and the period of time that the documentation should cover. They will also have to define roles and responsibilities, specifying who will conduct evaluations and how reviewers will be assigned. Finally, departments must specify what each evaluation component will produce and how these products will be used in different contexts (e.g., annual reviews, promotion and tenure decisions, or formative feedback for teaching improvement). For example, peer observations might result in a structured report, while self-reflection could take the form of an annual teaching statement or bulleted points.

Below, for each evaluation purpose or context, we provide several more specific questions to guide department design of the evaluation process, along with examples of department decisions about each one.

Instructor Representations of Teaching

For departments whose change effort centers on the way instructors document and represent their own teaching, project teams should decide on the following:

- What is the purpose of an instructor's representation of their teaching? How will self-reflection statements or supporting documentation be used within the annual or multiterm review process?

- What guidelines and structure will instructors be provided for generating self-reflective teaching statements?
- What is the focus of the self-reflective statement? What time frame will be covered? How many courses and dimensions of teaching will be addressed?
- What supporting documentation should be included, and how should it be organized?

For instance, the Department of English at KU has used the Benchmarks framework to develop a template for instructors to use in annual review. Instructors submit brief narrative statements about each defined dimension of teaching to document their teaching contributions from the previous year. Faculty are encouraged to select one course for their narrative as an illustration of their approaches to teaching. They are encouraged but not required to submit supporting documentation, and the template provides suggestions of materials that could be submitted as supplemental evidence. The KU Department of Educational Psychology has adopted a similar but streamlined approach that asks instructors to focus on a subset of two teaching dimensions each year. The UMass Department of Biochemistry and Molecular Biology has used the TEval dimensions to restructure their prompts for an annotated annual review of teaching form to gather details about faculty teaching and mentoring.

Peer or Third-Party Review

For peer or third-party reviews, key considerations include the following:

- What is the purpose and product of the peer or third-party review process? Is it to generate feedback to improve teaching, or will it generate evidence for summative evaluation? If so, what form will that evidence take?
- What is the focus of the evaluation? Which dimensions of teaching should be considered?

- How often are instructors expected to be reviewed or observed? How might this vary for instructors at different career levels and in different instructional roles?
- For peer reviews, what time frame should be covered (e.g., a single course offering, an instructor's teaching over the past year)?
- Who will conduct peer reviews? How will the reviewer role be assigned, and what guidance will be provided?
- For third-party observations, what observation tool will be used? How many observations will be carried out, in what time frame?

For instance, the Department of Linguistics at KU adapted the Benchmarks rubric and peer review protocol to restructure and bring consistency to peer reviews. They developed a schedule and expectations for peer review of individual courses (e.g., yearly for faculty in their first three years, every other year thereafter) and a process for chair assignment of peer reviewers with the expectation that every faculty member will participate in the process at least every few years. The use of the rubric for the peer review provides guidance and consistency for the process. Reviewers complete the rubric and annotate it with constructive comments. This product is returned as feedback to the instructor and submitted as evidence in promotion and tenure dossiers. The Linguistics Department at UMass also focused on peer review in its change effort but only for formative purposes to foster dialogue about teaching and improvement. In its model, faculty opted in to participate in peer review triads or dyads that met midsemester to provide feedback on teaching.

Summative Evaluations: Promotion and Tenure, Reappointment, or Merit Review

To design processes for summative evaluations like promotion, tenure, and merit reviews, departments should consider questions such as the following:

- What forms of evidence and artifacts from each of the three lenses should be included in candidates' dossiers?

- What is the focus of the evaluation? What time frame should be covered by the evaluation activity? How many courses and how many dimensions of teaching should be considered?
- What guidance or templates for materials preparation will be provided to candidates? Peer reviewers?
- What criteria will be used to evaluate the dossier? In addition to defining what effective teaching "looks like" at different levels of proficiency (as described under "Defining Effective Teaching"), departments will also need to identify expectations for achievement of the rubric levels for evaluation purposes.
- How will criteria be communicated to candidates?
- Who will conduct the evaluation, and what products will be generated?
- How will evaluators be prepared to apply the criteria to candidates' materials?

Some of these questions may already be addressed in departmental bylaws or institutional policy, whereas others will need to be determined by the department team. Illustrating some of these design decisions, the CU Department of History used the TEval framework to redesign a peer course-level evaluation system that all instructors in the department participate in. They also redesigned the promotion, tenure, and reappointment (PTR) process for tenure-line and teaching faculty so that it draws on evidence from peer course evaluation letters, student surveys of teaching, and self-reflection narratives. Criteria for evaluation are articulated in a rubric that is available to faculty members and used by the PTR committee to evaluate these materials for promotion, tenure, and reappointment.

The KU Department of Chemical and Petroleum Engineering also developed new processes for peer review that contribute artifacts to promotion, tenure, and annual review. All faculty are assigned to a peer triad or quad that meets periodically throughout the year, and at the end of the year, the group produces a collective report that is submitted to a teaching evaluation committee. Faculty members also submit reflection narratives and a student survey of teaching results. The teaching evaluation committee uses an adapted version of the Benchmarks rubric to review the materials and submits a recommended rating on each dimension of the rubric to the promotion and tenure committee and the department chair (for annual review). Using performance criteria developed by the department, the committee and/or chair provide the rating of the faculty member's teaching for summative evaluation purposes.

In addition to specifying the processes through which evidence will be collected and reviewed for formative or summative evaluation, department teams will also need to consider how the proposed processes will align with existing structures for annual merit, reappointment, promotion, and tenure systems. In the TEval project, several departments developed comprehensive evaluation systems. Teams should also review and adhere to departmental policies when implementing new teaching evaluation practices and identify any governance steps at the department, school, or institutional levels (e.g., committee approvals, department-wide votes) that are required for the official adoption of new evaluation tools or processes.

Implementing and Monitoring New Methods

Once departments have developed processes for the use of new frameworks and tools for documenting and evaluating teaching effectiveness, they are ready to put the plan into action. For departments that have focused on adopting particular tools or dimensions of an evaluation system but have not yet developed a completely revamped evaluation system, we suggest that they pilot those new tools or processes to gather input and generate broad engagement. Unless a department is implementing new tools and processes that have been used heavily by other units and have a high level of readiness for change, even department teams that have developed a comprehensive new evaluation system might consider starting with a pilot. Many departments in the TEval project, including the Department of History at CU and the Chemical and Petroleum Engineering Department at KU, adopted this approach, which allowed for lower-stakes testing and refinement of approaches while cultivating broader support. This approach could also enable departments to test their processes while they are working to gather any necessary approvals at the department, school, or institutional level.

It will also be important for department teams to actively monitor the new processes as they are being implemented, making minor course corrections if needed and noting refinements for the next iteration. This involves identifying key stakeholders to provide feedback on the new processes and establishing mechanisms to collect feedback from department members who are using the new tools and processes, communicating with key stakeholders about the benefits of the new approaches and addressing concerns, and developing strategies to cultivate broader departmental support for the new processes. For instance, positive feedback from members of the CU History Department in response to a survey on pilot implementation smoothed the way for the department's vote for full adoption of the new processes.

Engaging in Iteration and Continuous Improvement

Our model for department-level change, with its grounding in theories of organizational learning and continuous improvement, posits that effective approaches to meaningful and sustainable transformation involve ongoing refinement and adaptation.[15] Thus, departments should plan to engage in regular review and iterative adjustments based on feedback from department members; attention to the outcomes of the process; and changing needs, priorities, and educational trends within the department or institution. A commitment to iteration and continuous improvement follows from our recommendation to begin with a pilot of new processes. For many departments in the TEval initiative, later iterations were intentionally designed to build on the successes demonstrated in initial iterations, broadening the scale and scope of the initial effort. Our recommendations for implementing new methods emphasize the importance of monitoring the results and gathering feedback from key stakeholders. Thus, department teams will need to develop a systematic approach to incorporating such feedback and making adjustments to the processes after the initial implementation.

But the focus on feedback and refinement should not end with a pilot project, as iteration and continuous improvement are also essential to ensuring the long-term effectiveness and relevance of the department's approaches. To this end, departments should establish a feedback loop that provides opportunities for faculty input and creates a regular schedule for reviewing and revising the teaching evaluation system. That way, they can assess how well the tools and processes align with department needs and goals for teaching and student learning. Additional suggestions include encouraging ongoing discussion within the department about teaching quality and evaluation to keep faculty engaged with the process and staying informed of developments in teaching evaluation practice in higher education to inform future modifications. Adjustments might include modifying the definition and criteria for teaching effectiveness, changing the weights of different factors to better align with department priorities, and incorporating new forms of evidence. For instance, several departments in the TEval project found that they had underspecified the criteria for mentoring and advising and thus needed to further articulate their expectations in later iterations of their work.

Identifying Key Supports for the Departmental Change Process

Earlier we discussed the value of proactively identifying facilitating factors and potential barriers at the outset of a teaching evaluation reform initiative. Identifying resources for support throughout the change process is equally important. These supports can help enhance the efficiency and quality of department change efforts and help departments navigate friction and maintain momentum. We list here a variety of resources that exist at most universities and colleges. We remind change leaders of the usefulness of Bolman and Deal's four lenses (structural, human resources, political, and symbolic) as a way to brainstorm what faculty might most need. They can then assess resources available at their own institutions and consider how different resources would be helpful in different ways. There are a number of resources that departments might be able to utilize in parallel with the change process outlined above:

- *Frameworks, rubrics, toolkits*: As emphasized throughout this section, established frameworks like those described in chapter 1 can provide substantial scaffolding for the department change process. By adapting these frameworks to fit department needs and context, department teams can save time and ensure a scholarly foundation for their approaches.
- *Support for faculty time and effort*: Department change efforts take time and effort. By offering incentives like summer stipends or teaching or service credit, departments can honor the investment and commitment of team members and address a common barrier to change—lack of time. Departments might also consider other forms of support, such as funding for student or staff assistance, to reduce the time burden involved in change.
- *External resources*: On many campuses, there are support structures outside the department, such as teaching and learning centers, that can offer expertise, consulting, and professional development opportunities that keep department members apprised of new approaches to documenting and representing teaching and to evaluation. Relatedly, departments could work with external facilitators (who may or may not be affiliated with a teaching center) who can guide departmental discussions and provide objective perspectives. Each campus involved in TEval relied on some level of external facilitation of the department change process. At KU, a faculty fellow and leaders from

the teaching center served as liaisons or consultants to the departments; at UMass, consultative support came from an associate dean who was the leader of the campus-wide initiative; and at CU, this support came from postdoctoral fellows employed by the central project team.

- *Models and exemplars*: Teaching evaluation models from other departments or institutions can provide valuable insights and inspiration for department teams. Opportunities to learn about both the successes and challenges faced by others can help departments anticipate potential issues and adapt tested strategies to their specific context. For instance, several departments in the TEval project found it helpful to review and adapt peer observation protocols or self-reflection prompts that had been successfully implemented in other disciplines or institutions.
- *Communities of transformation*: Engaging with broader communities focused on the transformation of teaching evaluation can provide department team members with valuable social support and opportunities for idea exchange and shared problem-solving. In the TEval project, we convened campus-wide communities or stakeholder groups on each campus to create a platform for sense-making, sense-giving, and sharing of ideas about how to navigate common challenges. We also developed a multi-institutional network and convened regular cross-institutional meetings and workshops to provide even broader perspectives and support.

The various supports described above also reinforce one another. The availability of well-developed frameworks, exemplars, and structural supports can significantly reduce the time and effort required for departments embarking on change initiatives. As more departments engage in this work, the collective knowledge base will grow, helping to streamline the process for subsequent adopters. This compounding effect was evident in the TEval project. Later cohorts of departments benefitted from the groundwork laid by earlier participants as well as the proliferation of tools and resources that TEval leaders developed in response to the needs of participating departments. For instance, at KU, a recent cohort of departments that was recruited specifically to develop new models for the annual review of teaching was able to design, implement, and evaluate their models on an accelerated timeline (a single academic year) relative to previous cohorts. Thus, as the ecosystem of support for teaching evaluation reform grows richer, the barrier of time and effort—often a significant deterrent to change—becomes increasingly manageable.

DEPARTMENT SCENARIOS: ILLUSTRATING THE CHANGE PROCESS IN ACTION

Having outlined our model for department-level transformation, we now return to our three illustrative scenarios to examine how these change processes unfold in specific departmental contexts. The goal is to see how the steps of defining effective teaching, identifying evidence, developing evaluation systems, implementing changes, and refining approaches manifest in real department settings.

Scenario 1: History at CU

The CU History Department's change story exemplifies how a high level of readiness can lead to meaningful improvement of high-stakes, summative evaluations of teaching. The process involved identifying and supporting a team to adapt external frameworks to their context, resulting in a holistic system that comprehensively defined teaching effectiveness and provided structure for peer review and self-reflection. The department used a pilot implementation to generate support for the system among department members. Success in securing full faculty approval demonstrates effective consensus-building, which occurred formally through faculty-wide discussions and informally through one-on-one discussions. The department's engagement with broader communities, including campus-wide stakeholder dialogues and the TEval network, provided valuable support and learning opportunities. The department was well-positioned to respond to new standards adopted by the College of Arts and Sciences after they had begun their department-level change process. Notably, the department's strategic alignment of teaching evaluation reform with accreditation preparation showcases how such initiatives can serve multiple institutional goals simultaneously, enhancing the value of the work and contributing to greater efficiency in department processes.

Scenario 2: Chemical and Petroleum Engineering at KU

The work of the Department of Chemical and Petroleum Engineering at KU illustrates the effectiveness of a phased approach in building capacity and support for broader change. The department's strategy of starting with formative evaluation through peer review triads before expanding to summative processes allowed it to address immediate needs while gradually building interest in and documentation of the success and value of newer approaches. Their use of existing structures, such as a mentoring committee, and external resources like the Center for Teaching Excellence, provided a strong foundation for the department's efforts. They also leveraged faculty champions for the approaches being advanced and participated in broader communities to support idea exchange. The department's success in moving from a small group of volunteers focused on mentoring and formative peer review to department-wide implementation of a comprehensive system for holistic, multisource evaluation over three years demonstrates how iteration and the generation of visible benefits can secure buy-in. A combination of disruptors—department leadership change, an emergent department need, and an opportunity to compete for external recognition—served as a catalyst for a new phase that scaled the reform effort to department-wide implementation of a comprehensive teaching evaluation system based on the TEval approach.

Scenario 3: Linguistics at UMass

The experience of the UMass Linguistics Department highlights the value of flexible implementation in the face of institutional constraints. The department built on existing strengths, including a strong teaching culture and a previously developed educational effectiveness plan. They focused on a specific evaluation purpose, namely midterm, formative peer reviews, that aligned well with departmental needs and interests. The department used small-scale implementation, forming two triads to test and refine their approaches. Although other demands associated with the COVID-19 pandemic eventually led to a pause in the formal triad approach, the department's continued use of TEval resources for faculty mentoring demonstrates the lasting impact of even partial implementation. This case shows how departments can make meaningful progress in improving teaching evaluation, even when unable to pursue comprehensive reform, and how such efforts can enhance departmental knowledge and capacity for future initiatives.

IMPORTANT POINTS TO TAKE FROM THIS CHAPTER

We conclude this chapter by elevating some key lessons learned and cross-cutting recommendations for department leaders to keep in mind when launching and leading a department-level change initiative.

- *Attend to local context*: There is no one-size-fits-all solution for transforming teaching evaluation. Successful change efforts at the department level will build upon existing strengths and past initiatives related to teaching excellence. Departments should choose their initial focus and tailor their approaches based on their specific needs and readiness. Whereas some departments might successfully dive into a comprehensive revamping of their evaluation systems, others may start with one dimension of the evaluation process and adopt a phased approach to build interest, demonstrate the value of new approaches, and progressively expand to more comprehensive changes.

- *Prioritize communication and consensus building*: Throughout the change process, maintain transparent and consistent communication with the entire department. Identify regular opportunities, such as faculty meetings or retreats, during which the department team or leadership can update faculty colleagues on the team's work and elicit input. Use collaborative decision-making approaches to foster a shared vision and support ongoing consensus-building. Cultivate champions across different faculty groups and encourage peer learning. Frame the change effort as a shared journey toward educational excellence to create a culture of continuous improvement and collective ownership of the evaluation process.
- *Recognize that change takes time and iteration*: The change literature and our research in the TEval project show that meaningful change takes time and often requires multiple iterations. Be patient, allow for adjustments, and celebrate small victories to maintain momentum. A phased approach allows departments to learn from early implementations, refine their processes based on feedback and experience, and gradually build support and expertise among faculty members.
- *Strive for alignment and synergy across processes*: Develop evaluation processes that align with institutional priorities and can serve multiple purposes, ensuring that activities and products generated for one purpose (e.g., faculty reflection on student learning or evaluation) can contribute to other processes (e.g., degree outcomes assessment or academic program review). This integrative approach not only reinforces the value of evaluation processes but also improves efficiency by reducing redundant efforts, thereby maximizing the impact of the activities while minimizing the burden on both faculty and administrators.

- *Cultivate champions and allies*: Identify and support champions both within and outside of the department who can advocate for the change. Communicate strong backing from department leadership and work to build a critical mass of engaged faculty. Develop allies in other departments, university administration, and governance to broaden awareness of transformed approaches and help navigate institutional barriers and approvals.
- *Leverage external resources*: Use external frameworks, tools, and expertise to guide the process and provide objective perspectives. Take part in external networks and communities organized around teaching evaluation reform. These interactions with peers can influence social norms within the department, shape change narratives, and introduce new ideas and resources.
- *Commit to continuous improvement*: Establish mechanisms for ongoing assessment, reflection, and refinement of new practices and be prepared to adjust approaches based on feedback and outcomes. Design the process itself to be dynamic with built-in occasions to revisit and possibly refine the department's system to ensure that it continues to serve the department's goals and emerging issues in higher education.
- *Attend to and address practical challenges*: Acknowledge and proactively address time constraints, potential resistance, and resource limitations that can get in the way of teaching evaluation reform. Invite skeptical faculty to take part in the design process. Consider providing incentives or recognition for participation in the initiative to encourage engagement and signal the department's commitment.
- *Plan for sustainability*: Design processes and structures that can be maintained beyond the initial change effort, particularly if the change effort is supported by a temporary resource infusion such as a grant or support from an external facilitator. This includes succession planning for leadership roles and integrating new practices into departmental policies.

- *Adopt a systems view*: As we emphasize throughout this book, departmental change exists within a broader institutional context. Thus, the transformation of teaching evaluation must be carried out with an eye toward the whole institutional system. Systems approaches underscore the need for department leaders to seek connections with other levels of the system and multiple stakeholder groups to see and support change.

4

Considerations for Senior Institutional Leaders

EXPERIENCED LEADERS RECOGNIZE THE challenge of changing an organization as complex as a university or a college. A top-down approach to change can work in some circumstances, but it runs the risk of alienating independent-minded faculty members, department chairs, and deans. That's why we advocate a systems approach, which allows leaders to consider how the many components of a university or college structure might be employed to effect change. In this chapter, we focus on how senior leaders can apply that systems approach to changing the evaluation of teaching. Campus administrative leaders hold positions that enable them to make strategic moves and decisions that affect the institution as a system. They are well-positioned to assess the issues, policies, and practices that need attention at each organizational level. They can convene stakeholders and those at different levels of the institution to discuss transforming teaching evaluation. Departmental efforts to change teaching evaluation are unlikely to succeed unless institutional leaders recognize the broader system in which such work is occurring and ensure support at all levels of the institution and from an array of stakeholders.

Building on the discussion in chapter 2 on theories, frameworks, and principles related to systemic change in higher education, this chapter outlines seven specific practical strategies that senior institutional leaders can take to support and advance the reform of teaching evaluation. Each of these strategies is informed by the research on change in complex organizations. In chapter 2, we also explained how and why a coordinated top-down, bottom-up, middle-out approach works well to advance change in universities and colleges. In chapter 3, we took a deep dive into the central role of departments in changing teaching evaluation, including the kind of leadership that department chairs need to provide. We emphasized that the department is typically the central location for the significant collaborative work needed to change teaching evaluation since the work of faculty as teachers is situated within departmental structures and cultures. However, senior institutional leaders—such as provosts, vice provosts, deans, and teaching center directors—also are critically important to efforts to change teaching evaluation.

We have presented these strategies in a straightforward way for ease of reading and reference as you engage in your change work. However, we emphasize that these strategies are not intended to be read as linear steps (although, as presented below, some may naturally be most helpful earlier in a change process and others later in the process). Rather, institutional leaders should consider these strategies as an integrated and complementary set; that is, they are not mutually exclusive, and they complement and strengthen one another. Leaders can and should engage with more than one at a time. As discussed in chapter 2, systemic change work to advance a transformational goal requires the use of multiple strategies and attention to multiple levels of the organization—and these are likely to change over time and institutional circumstances. Specific challenges addressed and tactics used sometimes appear in multiple strategies. We don't see this as redundancy. Rather, we argue that a systems view may lead to leveraging activities in multiple, high-value ways.

LEADERSHIP STRATEGY 1: SITUATE EFFORTS TO CHANGE TEACHING EVALUATION WITHIN THE SPECIFIC INSTITUTIONAL CONTEXT

In both chapters 2 and 3, we discussed the importance of assessing institutional readiness to change as well as examining institutional culture and context as part of deciding how to proceed with a major change initiative. Institutional leaders can help convene department chairs and others working directly on transforming teaching to discuss readiness and fruitful paths forward. They can also connect efforts to improve teaching evaluation with other institutional goals and initiatives. Provost, deans, and teaching center directors can be particularly strategic in making these connections by developing a narrative that provides a rationale for the values and importance of the change work.

Align the Change Project with Other Campus Goals and Priorities

Colleges and universities typically have multiple projects and initiatives supporting student learning and success. Efforts to improve teaching evaluation contribute to the broader goal of ensuring excellence in teaching and positive student outcomes. Thus, when institutional leaders align an initiative to improve teaching evaluation with institutional priorities to bolster student success and strengthen faculty effectiveness, they create a powerful argument in support of the change initiative. For example, at the University of Kansas (KU), leaders of the TEval project explicitly built on earlier institutional work and departmental projects to reenergize the undergraduate curriculum. Some departments elected to become involved because they had enjoyed and benefited from the earlier curricular work, trusted the Center for Teaching Excellence (which facilitated both change projects), and wanted to further expand the impact of their earlier work. The teaching evaluation initiative also aligned well with interest among senior institutional leaders in improving the annual review process for faculty. At the University of Massachusetts Amherst (UMass), the faculty union has been interested in ways to improve and strengthen teaching evaluation as a factor in creating a more robust faculty reward system. Situating the teaching evaluation project in relationship to union priorities attracted faculty interest and support for the change efforts.

Develop a Narrative

Provosts and deans are well-positioned to develop and articulate a narrative that shows how work on teaching evaluation relates to institutional priorities. They know the overarching institutional priorities and can explain how efforts to transform teaching evaluation relate to and support those priorities. TEval leaders at UMass have encouraged faculty to perceive their work to improve teaching evaluation as part of an overarching institutional goal to support student learning. At KU, the director of the Center for Teaching Excellence has linked the TEval project to earlier institutional work on making teaching more visible, thus positioning the current work as a logical next step, especially for the many departments and faculty who were involved previously.

Many narratives are possible. Here, we offer three examples of possible frameworks that can help engage faculty in the improvement of teaching evaluation. These narratives, which can be interwoven, each provide powerful messages to motivate faculty efforts to strengthen and improve teaching evaluation and can be connected to other institutional priorities.

The Need to Address Shortcomings in Typical Approaches to Teaching Evaluation

This narrative resonates with faculty who believe that the assessment of the quality of teaching requires more than student perspectives. The biases that can influence student feedback also concern faculty members who may perceive that, on the basis of their gender or race, the scheduled time of their class, or the positioning of their course as a requirement or an elective, student ratings may be skewed. Teaching involves a range of duties, such as preparing a syllabus, conferring with students, and situating a course within the broader departmental curriculum. These dimensions are often not factored into the teaching evaluation process. Another faculty concern is that the career stages of instructors are not typically considered when assessing teaching expertise. Faculty may also want to be more innovative in how student voices are integrated into their efforts to assess and improve their teaching. Institutional leaders can tap into this skepticism and encourage involvement in transforming teaching evaluation as a way to address faculty concerns.

The Importance of Elevating Teaching as a Core Institutional Value

This narrative emphasizes that teaching—and, more specifically, student learning—is at the heart of academe. As such, efforts to discuss the characteristics of good teaching and to enable faculty to share, observe, and critique one another's approaches help to elevate the core institutional commitment to excellent teaching. Specific work around teaching evaluation helps improve the evaluation process but also keeps teaching excellence front and center for everyone at the institution.

Evaluation as a Tool to Improve the Quality of Teaching

If excellent teaching is indeed a key institutional commitment, then attention to effective evaluation approaches has the practical value of strengthening teaching practice. A compelling narrative can emphasize that better teaching evaluation processes can help instructors identify areas where changes could enhance student learning, develop specific ideas for making improvements, and then monitor and assess those changes and their impact—all with the support of interested colleagues.

This narrative also recognizes work to strengthen teaching that may already be occurring on campus but not fully acknowledged or rewarded.

These narratives may also be coupled with outward-facing responses to the public as a tool for acknowledging higher education's critical role in society and how we are assuming responsibility for our core missions and unique capacities to educate the breadth and diversity of learners in our systems.

LEADERSHIP STRATEGY 2: RECOGNIZE AND MANAGE THE CHANGE PROCESS OVER TIME

Significant change takes time. Long-term change endeavors also are dynamic, moving through stages that require change leaders to shift strategies over time. Institutional leaders encouraging systemic change should work with the long view in mind. At least three stages are typical in such projects (as readers will recall from chapter 2): getting started, selecting and implementing interventions and strategies, and sustaining the change. Within each stage, change leaders may need to address different tasks and issues as they strive to develop more effective, authentic, equitable, and useful teaching evaluation processes. Here, we refer to the sequential stages of advancing transformational change that we explained in chapter 2 and indicate specific issues and tasks that leaders (especially those in institution-wide leadership roles) need to consider.

Getting Started

In this early stage, change leaders (both institutional leaders and department chairs) need to examine the context and culture they want to change and begin to articulate a vision. Examining the context involves analyzing the current approach to teaching evaluation, articulating what is problematic about current evaluation processes, and explaining why a change is needed. This stage may also involve identifying key issues at the institution relevant to the intended change process and the institution's history that can help situate the new effort within institutional values or history. At KU, for example, leaders of the TEval project reminded colleagues of the institution's history and earlier projects to make teaching more visible, and they situated the new work on teaching evaluation in the context of ongoing institutional priorities. At the department level, as mentioned in chapter 3, the initiation stage includes conversations on who will be involved (early-career faculty, for instance, or all faculty) and where to begin (e.g., small groups trying out peer review and developing self-assessment guidelines or using a rubric to develop portfolios for annual review).

Selecting and Implementing Strategies

At this stage, the work is underway and gaining traction. Several tasks are important. Those leading the change effort around teaching evaluation need to motivate faculty interest and commitment, create connections with an array of institutional leaders and allies, build capacity and engagement, and manage barriers and resistance. Most organizational change endeavors struggle to move from the involvement of a few early adopters to greater faculty engagement. To address this challenge in the transformation of teaching evaluation, leaders can show faculty members how changing teaching evaluation relates to their natural interest in teaching, supports the entire breadth of faculty on campus, and creates networks that link colleagues who share interests in teaching.

In addition to cultivating faculty commitment, institutional change leaders should seek connections with others who share their goals. Strategies to create such connections include actively seeking and cultivating supportive leaders at several organizational levels, including departments and colleges, identifying allies across the institution whose own priorities are also relevant to reforming teaching evaluation, hosting town hall discussions, and looking for potential champions who are deeply committed to transforming teaching evaluation. At KU, the director and associate director of the teaching center were purposeful in targeting potential allies (such as a vice provost whose portfolio included faculty-related policies) and visiting them to discuss the TEval project goals. Senior-level institutional leaders can also advance the work by ensuring that resources are available for those engaged in the change work and that institutional promotion processes take into account faculty time and effort invested in such work.

Managing barriers is another important task in this stage. Certain barriers are common: avoidance by faculty members who worry that the task is too overwhelming; time constraints; and faculty uncertainty about institutional commitment, including whether institutional tenure and promotion processes will accommodate new approaches to teaching evaluation. Developing strategies to address these barriers, such as frequent and transparent communication, acknowledging difficulties, providing resources (material, intellectual, and financial), cultivating leadership at all levels, and celebrating early successes, is an important way that senior institutional leaders can help support and advance change in teaching evaluation.

Sustaining the Change over Time

As a new approach to evaluating teaching becomes embedded into regular faculty work, senior leaders play an important role in maintaining institutional commitment. They can nurture that commitment by communicating the benefits and successes in departments, ensuring that the new approaches are valued in university promotion reviews, and acknowledging, rewarding, and celebrating those who have invested time and energy into the change process. Understanding the stages of a change initiative can help senior leaders make strategic decisions about where their time and effort will be most useful.

LEADERSHIP STRATEGY 3: MOTIVATE FACULTY TO JOIN EFFORTS TO TRANSFORM TEACHING EVALUATION

Change leaders must develop multiple, interlocking strategies to move an institution toward a goal. Looking at the organization through different frames (the structural frame, political frame, symbolic frame, and human resources frame) can help leaders identify a potentially powerful set of strategies. (We explain those in chapter 2, along with the importance of taking a top-down, middle-out, and bottom-up approach to transforming teaching evaluation.) The human resources frame draws attention to the faculty, which is central to developing new approaches to teaching evaluation. Faculty and the work they do are at the heart of universities and colleges, so their "bottom-up" work is essential to the success of changing teaching evaluation. Yet faculty have many other responsibilities and tugs on their time, so senior leaders must approach the change process strategically.

As provosts, deans, and teaching center directors set institutional agendas, lead meetings, and frame the priorities of the institution, they can use their positions as platforms to communicate and motivate change efforts. That includes encouraging faculty members and administrators to invest time and energy in transforming teaching evaluation. Senior institutional leaders and department chairs can draw on several issues of interest to faculty members: the strong commitment to teaching felt by many faculty, the natural inclination of faculty to enjoy talking with their colleagues about issues of common interest, concern about how time spent on teaching is handled in promotion and reward processes, and worries about limitations and biases that often appear in student evaluation surveys.

Build on Faculty Members' Interest in Talking About Their Work as Teachers

As faculty members fulfill an array of daily responsibilities, they typically have little opportunity to discuss what good teaching looks like. Senior institutional leaders can invite faculty members into such discussions and encourage parallel opportunities within departments. Talking about what constitutes good teaching elevates the value of teaching within the institution, potentially centering teaching at the heart of higher education. Deans and teaching center directors can encourage faculty members to consider how learning occurs in their specific fields, how teaching practices can more fully support effective learning for the full array of students, and what defines effective versus less effective teaching in a specific field. Departments that discuss their beliefs and practices around good teaching deepen their collective values. For example, deeper commitment to supporting students as learners may emerge in such discussions, leading faculty participants to think more fully about their roles in promoting institutional priorities around diversity, equity, and inclusion. For many faculty members, such conversations about their work as teachers are intrinsically rewarding and energizing.

Emphasize That Improved Evaluation Can Acknowledge and Elevate the Work of Faculty as Teachers

Administrative leaders can encourage faculty to join efforts to reform teaching evaluation as a way to better recognize the wide array of work encompassing effective teaching. This includes working on curriculum development, identifying resources to support learning, assessing learning outcomes, providing feedback, and engaging in course revision. Promotion and tenure processes at many universities have historically undervalued the teaching elements of faculty work. Making good teaching visible and exploring the often-hidden efforts of educational practice through more holistic evaluation elevates that work. This is especially important for teaching faculty, who often feel undervalued and overlooked. Early-career faculty who are investing significant time in establishing themselves as teachers also benefit from evaluation processes that highlight the depth and extent of their work.

Senior leaders can also point out that a multidimensional evaluation process enriches the information available for promotion and tenure considerations. More holistic approaches to teaching evaluation that include peer observation and self-reflection provide expanded perspectives that instructors can use to better support student learning. Such feedback is especially useful to faculty members striving to learn to teach effectively in online and hybrid courses.

Another strategy to attract faculty interest is to connect efforts to improve teaching evaluation to other faculty concerns. For example, in history departments, faculty may be concerned about the "crisis of the humanities" and the associated patterns of declining enrollments. The chair of the history department at one of our universities made an argument that excellent teaching attracts students and that efforts to improve the evaluation of teaching could strengthen the department's reputation by showing that the faculty members care about good teaching.

Highlight How Change in Teaching Evaluation Can Address Long-Standing Critiques

Provosts, deans, and teaching center directors can remind faculty of the concerns often expressed about reliance on student surveys for evaluating teaching. One-time surveys of students do not capture the many dimensions involved in effective teaching, including preparation, efforts to stay abreast of the field, feedback to students, collaboration with other colleagues to ensure a cohesive curriculum, and course revision. Students do not have the disciplinary expertise to comment with knowledge on many aspects of faculty teaching activities, such as whether the course content is comprehensive, up-to-date, and appropriate. Many instructors feel that their work as teachers is not fully visible or recognized, and, therefore, that evaluation based solely on student surveys is superficial and even capricious. Furthermore, bias based on gender, race or ethnicity, appearance, or other personal factors can easily enter into typical student-based evaluation processes. When an institution embarks on developing a new approach to teaching evaluation, institution-level change leaders can motivate involvement by inviting colleagues to help create more equitable, inclusive, and useful ways to evaluate teaching. The University of Colorado Boulder provides a good example. When the faculty assembly recommended doing away with the omnibus ratings (rate the professor and course on a 1–5 scale), and the administration followed suit, it was unclear how the remaining student ratings could be used in faculty evaluation. Faculty and academic leaders working on a Teaching Quality Framework provided useful approaches that supported departments in their continued use of student ratings to contribute to meaningful evaluation of their faculty. Some departments identified and tracked specific sets of questions that they noted aligned with program goals, often looking for change over time in these measures for their instructors. Other departments coupled the use of student ratings with the peer review process, where, as part of the review, an instructor and reviewer would determine which questions were most applicable to the course being reviewed. Faculty were able to decide what information and processes would be of most use to them and their departments to make student ratings as useful as possible.

LEADERSHIP STRATEGY 4: IDENTIFY, CONNECT, AND CONVENE KEY LEADERS AND ALLIES ACROSS THE INSTITUTION

The political theories and the political frame for understanding an institution, discussed in chapter 2, suggest that finding allies is an important strategy in advancing a change goal. Provosts, deans, and teaching center directors can help identify and connect leaders across campus whose expertise and positions lend credibility, strength, and focus to change efforts. Approaches to changing teaching evaluation are most effective when leaders at various organizational levels are involved.

Convene Key Leaders and Allies Across the Institution

Organizational change efforts benefit from wide support. Provosts and deans have a broad perspective that enables them to consider who across the institution can help change teaching evaluation. They also typically enjoy sufficient influence to encourage other campus leaders to take notice and to identify and enlist potential allies. For example, institutional leaders for diversity, equity, and inclusion may be good allies. These colleagues may see new approaches to documenting teaching practices as a path toward increased recognition of the diverse ways in which individual faculty members contribute to the collective good. Some institutions have councils of associate deans who work on personnel matters or groups of instructors in fixed-term positions who have extensive teaching assignments. Both of these groups would constitute potentially effective allies to those working on transforming teaching evaluation. As mentioned, the faculty union at UMass had a strong interest in faculty evaluation and made a productive and supportive ally in initiating, developing, and sustaining the change efforts around teaching evaluation.

The University of Kansas and its Benchmarks initiative (the local name of KU's project to transform teaching evaluation) provides a good example of how connection and collaboration among leaders at different institutional levels and roles can advance efforts to change teaching evaluation. The Center for Teaching Excellence (CTE) played a central role in providing scaffolding for the project by convening departmental leaders, offering rubrics and examples, and providing consultative support to individual departments. The deep work of considering how to apply the TEval framework to faculty work occurred within each department, where faculty and administrative change leaders chose where to focus initial efforts. Some departments focused on annual review, others on evaluations for promotion; some focused on teaching assistants or pretenure faculty, while others included all faculty. The CTE built on that department-level work by ensuring that occasions and structures were in place to discuss resources, foster exchange of ideas, and encourage discussion of challenges among department chairs and other leaders. Alongside that work, the vice provost for faculty affairs publicly supported the Benchmarks project and integrated elements of it into institutional evaluation processes for teaching faculty. Collaboration across institutional levels and units creates an environment in which messages, policies, and actions around teaching evaluation can be aligned and mutually reinforcing.

Identify Institutional Change Champions

In addition to facilitating collaboration across grassroots, midlevel, and top-level leaders, senior institutional leaders can identify "champions" who are committed to the vision and the process of achieving a vision. In our studies of effective campus change, we saw examples of such champions at both the department and college levels—individuals motivated by their commitment to high-quality teaching and their belief that teaching evaluation can be an effective way to elevate and improve teaching.

The discussion in chapter 3 showed how champions within departments tend to be faculty members who are dedicated teachers and see that effective evaluation can strengthen departmental teaching. Such departmental champions may serve as chairs of curriculum or promotion committees, or they may be respected instructors who articulate and model the values of good teaching. The voices of such faculty can attract the attention of colleagues who may choose to become involved out of their respect for these colleagues or who will at least support the work in a general way because they value and trust others assuming leadership for the work.

At the institutional level, champions are usually people who enjoy wide recognition, admiration, and trust. The role played by an institutional champion at the University of Colorado Boulder provides a good example. Many faculty members and institutional leaders who were interviewed as part of this project cited the impact of Professor Noah Finkelstein (one of the authors of this book) in framing the issues of importance and in igniting excitement about the possibilities for improving the quality of teaching through attention to teaching evaluation. He was adept at explaining the goals and plans for the project in ways that attracted interest from colleagues across fields and from several deans who promoted the work in their colleges. At other institutions that want to change teaching evaluation, a senior-level institutional leader might identify a similar well-respected faculty member and encourage their involvement with the initiative. While highlighting the important role such a champion can play, we also urge change facilitators to be aware of potential downsides. Associating a change initiative too closely with one individual runs the risk of making it fragile or political. If that person were to leave or to anger some constituencies, the initiative could stall.

Provide Facilitation and Guidance

Good ideas themselves do not generate effective actions and definable results. Provosts, deans, and teaching center directors can nurture teaching evaluation projects by finding and supporting facilitators of the work. The University of Colorado Boulder provided departments working on changes to teaching evaluation with facilitators who organized and guided department meetings, summarized faculty discussions and decisions, provided templates and examples, developed action plans, provided reminders to hold participants accountable for their commitments and intentions, and maintained vision and forward motion. While the departments involved in TEval at UMass generally worked independently on their teaching evaluation projects, periodically, the TEval leader (Professor Gabriela Weaver, one of this book's authors) met with departments to offer feedback and guidance relevant to their work. The KU Center for Teaching Excellence provides a third example of how facilitation can help. Professors Andrea Follmer Greenhoot and Doug Ward, two of the book's authors and the director and associate director of the teaching center, convened department leaders periodically to discuss their work; also, upon request, staff members of the CTE visited departments to provide more explicit support. Such facilitation can help departments manage the challenges of change work.

LEADERSHIP STRATEGY 5: PROVIDE RESOURCES THAT SUPPORT NEW APPROACHES TO TEACHING EVALUATION

Advancing a transformative change initiative requires the use of multiple strategies or levers. Here, we highlight some of the specific strategies for change that senior institutional leaders are especially well-positioned to encourage. (See chapter 2 for more discussion of how multiple strategies are needed to foster effective change.) Provosts, deans, and teaching center directors can support professional development that helps faculty members and department chairs gain the knowledge and skills needed to envision, create, and implement new evaluation approaches. They can ensure that institutional reward systems recognize and honor the time and work invested in transforming teaching evaluation, and they can find ways to recognize, honor, and celebrate the commitment of time and the work involved in developing and implementing new approaches to evaluation.

Encourage Use of Tools, Evidence, and Examples

Drawing from existing resources can make a change project less of a heavy lift. Such resources can be found through national initiatives such as the TEval project and from other institutions working toward the same goal. The TEval project team has developed numerous tools and resources to support more equitable and effective teaching evaluation, drawing from the work at the three participating institutions. As mentioned in chapter 1, these resources include rubrics that articulate expectations for a broad range of teaching activities, protocols to guide peer review of courses, and guides for self-reflection and use of the student voice. Other resources include department templates for annual reviews, mapping tools for aligning evidence and artifacts with teaching dimensions, sample evaluation portfolios, and comprehensive guidebooks, including department toolkits. The TEval project has also produced repositories of materials related to department adaptations and strategies and examples of how such strategies interact with departmental readiness and culture. All are available on the TEval website (www.TEval.net). Such tools and resources can be adapted to new settings or introduced as sources of inspiration to suggest possibilities, stimulate discussion, and encourage faculty and department leaders to develop their own materials.

Provide Time, Space, and Professional Development to Support Faculty Use of New Tools

Faculty are typically busy with an array of responsibilities and may not be able to take the time to delve into the resources available to them. Campus leaders can create opportunities for discussion and exchange of ideas, resources, and concerns. Such cross-department interaction and collaboration provide encouragement, support, and resources. Departments just starting the work of changing teaching evaluation can pursue their own goals and timelines while also benefiting from the efforts, artifacts, and outcomes of other academic units further along in the process. Materials, templates, and examples of how other departments have approached improvement in teaching evaluation offer inspiration and practical assistance. Collaborations can include periodic meetings of representatives from departments and cross-institutional teams working on teaching evaluation and joint projects between departments and a teaching center. Having a rubric available to help with peer review is useful. However, having a specific time when someone with experience explains how to use the rubric, what to do with the data collected, and how to display and describe those data can mean the difference between whether a resource is used or not.

Much of the work of changing teaching evaluation needs to occur at the department level, where faculty are engaged in their day-to-day work. In addition to convening departmental teams for cross-institutional exchanges of ideas, institutional leaders can assess departmental needs. Institutional resources could be used, for example, to provide release time for faculty members leading departmental efforts to rethink their approaches to teaching evaluation. Department chairs and faculty may not be familiar with ways to approach formative and summative evaluation as part of teaching evaluation. Provosts and deans could provide financial resources to send department chairs or faculty leaders to national meetings where teaching evaluation is discussed or to other institutions trying innovative approaches or working on teaching evaluation in specific disciplines. The Center for Teaching Excellence at the University of Kansas regularly convened teams from departments working on transforming teaching evaluation. At the meetings, the teaching center director and staff led discussion, provided support and guidance, and gathered feedback and ideas for new tools and resources. Faculty leaders and chairs who participated reported that these meetings were essential to supporting their work.

Incentivize and Reward the Time and Work Invested in Teaching Evaluation

Faculty members are reluctant to invest time in activities that they aren't sure the institution or those who evaluate them will value. Working on teaching evaluation can be such an activity. At a minimum, faculty members want to know that spending time on revising evaluation methods will not harm their own standing. Intrinsic values often motivate faculty members to engage in improving teaching, but clear signals that such work is valued and will be rewarded are crucial in sustaining change efforts. Messaging from provosts and deans is especially important. Faculty members need to know that leaders value their contributions to important institutional work, such as transforming teaching evaluation, and that their work will be well-received in promotion dossiers and annual reviews. For example, deans might make clear statements that the work involved in transforming and conducting teaching evaluation will count toward teaching responsibilities or service contributions in annual evaluations. Department chairs and directors of teaching centers also play important roles in encouraging faculty members to invest time in peer review, self-reflection, and committee work focused on teaching evaluation. Ultimately, though, provosts and deans are best positioned to articulate and clarify institutional priorities and standards.

Ensure Appropriate Financial Resources Are Available

Change work in higher education relies heavily on commitment of time from faculty members and department chairs, but financial resources are also important. That's where senior leaders can be especially helpful. Provosts and deans (and sometimes department chairs) can arrange budgets to accommodate special faculty assignments involving release time from teaching or other duties. Such release time, for example, can enable a faculty member to lead a departmental team to re-envision teaching evaluation and to design a pilot project to test developing ideas. Sending a team to a national meeting to learn more about changing teaching evaluation is another example of how financial resources can help foster change work. When senior-level leaders take the time to discuss with department-level change leaders how they can be most helpful and what financial resources might be needed, they support the change work in tangible ways and send important symbolic messages that the institution values the work.

Use Symbolic Levers to Convey the Importance of Changing Teaching Evaluation

Senior-level administrators may sometimes undervalue or overlook the importance of using symbolic messages to change institutional culture and practices. Strategic use of communications is one strategy for senior leaders to consider as part of a "change portfolio." Provosts and deans often send periodic letters to their faculty constituencies, highlighting institutional or school priorities, mentioning colleagues who are investing time in various projects, and outlining a vision for the future of the institution or unit. Senior leaders also hold regular meetings with the administrative leaders who report to them, and they often provide opening remarks at workshops, convenings, and conferences that bring together campus stakeholders. Each of these occasions is an opportunity for senior leaders to explain the importance of new approaches to teaching evaluation, delineate how this initiative explicitly aligns with and supports an institutional priority (such as greater evidence of student success or high-quality teaching), and mention the names of individuals contributing to this work. Such regularly communicated sentiments send strong signals about why the change initiative is important and how those who are working on it are valued. Events and celebrations constitute another symbolic lever that senior leaders may use. For example, celebratory dinners that recognize departments that have made considerable progress on developing and implementing new approaches to teaching evaluation and that foreground remarks from visitors doing inspiring work in this area are "lighthouse signals" telling the campus that this work is important, respected, and encouraged. These symbolic forms can be productively coupled with other strategies: information sharing, connecting to key actors, and such.

LEADERSHIP STRATEGY 6: MANAGE BARRIERS AND MONITOR PROGRESS IN TRANSFORMING TEACHING EVALUATION

An important part of sustaining change, as explored in chapter 2, is identifying and managing barriers and monitoring, tracking, and evaluating progress. In addition to providing support and resources, institutional leaders can also play an important role in reducing resistance to change in teaching evaluation and establishing processes for evaluating the work and progress toward the goal of approaching teaching evaluation in more holistic, equitable, and transparent ways. At least two types of barriers may arise: challenges to faculty buy-in and involvement, including faculty concerns about practical issues such as time and energy required, and uncertainties about long-term institutional commitment and sustainability. Departments need to address these issues directly, but provosts, deans, and teaching center directors are particularly important in framing institutional responses. Senior leaders also are the most likely administrators to have the resources to invest in systems or people who can help with tracking progress.

Handle Challenges to Faculty Buy-In and Involvement

Each of the three universities we studied faced similar challenges in acquiring faculty buy-in and commitment. Faculty often lack a shared understanding of what good teaching is, and they often disagree about the usefulness of teaching evaluation and the need to transform how teaching is evaluated. This lack of shared vision can make discussions of a new framework difficult. Furthermore, faculty members are often skeptical about using the same standards to evaluate teaching across disciplines, in graduate and undergraduate courses, and in online courses.

Another challenge is that faculty members interested in changing the evaluation system often have limited time and are concerned that a holistic approach to evaluating teaching will increase their workload. For example, the TEval system includes self-assessment and peer review. Faculty may question the effort required to add those elements to teaching evaluation if they cannot see ways to connect it to annual reviews and reviews for promotion. They may also worry that efforts to innovate in their teaching, such as integrating team-based learning into classes, will result in lower ratings from students—and thus, they may shy away from evaluation approaches that could shine a light on teaching efforts they would prefer not to emphasize. Furthermore, peer reviewers and instructors may have differing philosophical views about the field or about effective teaching, and instructors may fear such differences could undermine the evaluation of their teaching.

Department leaders must address those concerns directly, but senior institutional leaders can help. As already suggested, one strategy is to help frame the broader context by explaining why teaching evaluation is important, how evaluation processes relate to the larger issue of teaching quality, and why these issues are of high priority to the institution. Notably, faculty arrive at our institutions with a sense of commitment to education, and leaders can support and cultivate such sentiments. With such framing, senior leaders signal that investing time in transforming teaching evaluation is aligned with institutional priorities. In our study, one institutional leader suggested that leaders can frame the "transformation of the evaluation of teaching as a way to protect the faculty, to give them a way of making sure their teaching score or their evaluation based on teaching would be more fair." These points will resonate with some faculty; others may value hearing that efforts to reform teaching evaluation are central to strengthening institutional excellence and supporting learning.

In response to concerns about whether time spent on improving teaching evaluation will "count" in promotion processes, provosts and deans can discuss what is valued in tenure and promotion decisions. In particular, they can signal that significant faculty contributions to the institution, such as transforming how teaching is evaluated, are valued and recognized in promotion processes. Department chairs are important players in providing information about how faculty members will be reviewed and assessed. At the same time, faculty members are sure to look to senior institutional leaders for clear articulation of expectations, criteria for promotion, and explanations of how their contributions and accomplishments are viewed.

Address Uncertainties About Institutional Commitment

Faculty skepticism of long-term institutional commitment to valuing teaching and creating new strategies for teaching evaluation also serves as a barrier to institutional progress. This skepticism can take several forms. In the face of uncertainty about institutional plans, faculty scrutinize senior-level leaders' involvement and commitment. At one of the universities studied, faculty noted that strong faculty leadership in transforming teaching evaluation was coupled with weak institutional support. That led to the reluctance of some department chairs and faculty to invest much effort in the work. Gaining attention, interest, and commitment from senior-level administrators can be a challenge for faculty leaders working on changing teaching evaluation. Conversely, a clear and firm commitment from institutional leaders sends a compelling signal to faculty.

The incentive systems of many universities have historically emphasized research over teaching. How efforts to transform teaching evaluation would be counted in promotion and tenure processes and how new and broader forms of evidence of teaching quality would be integrated into institution-level tenure and promotion processes are issues on the minds of many faculty members. Even when institutional leaders signal support and enthusiasm for the work, faculty express concern that such commitment will not translate into positive promotion and tenure decisions. In fact, some faculty worry that the teaching evaluation rubric could be used against a faculty member in the promotion process, leading to an unwelcome focus on areas needing development. Faculty members' intrinsic interests in improving their teaching—and thus in engaging in different forms of evaluation—will be difficult to pursue if the extrinsic reward system emphasizes other priorities. Because teaching evaluation is connected to tenure and promotion, many faculty interviewed felt that a change in teaching evaluation would be difficult without structural changes and support from senior leaders. Stated more positively, senior-level administrators have a key role to play in emphasizing institutional priorities and values in promotion processes.

Uncertainty about whether efforts to change teaching evaluation can be sustained over time constitutes another barrier that can deter campus-wide involvement. Gaining faculty interest, securing administrative support, and changing policies may not be sufficient. Institutional culture—what is valued, how people act over time, where faculty invest time, what language is used to speak of priorities, how practices shift—needs to change, too. Provosts and deans, along with teaching center directors, can provide assurances that the effort to reform teaching evaluation will make a long-term difference. As we assert throughout this book, changing teaching evaluation is a process requiring a systemic approach that embeds the change into the fabric of institutional culture, processes, and practices. Senior leaders are best poised to articulate ongoing and long-term commitment to the goal.

Ensure Continuous Improvement Through Monitoring and Evaluation

In chapter 2, we discussed the use of continuous monitoring and evaluation as an element in advancing and sustaining a significant change initiative. Leaders at all levels—department chairs, provosts, and deans—who are encouraging efforts to improve teaching evaluation should consider their role in continuous improvement efforts. Senior institutional leaders can encourage institution-level monitoring. Questions to consider include which departments are involved, how far along in their work each unit is, what common barriers departments and colleges encounter, and what support and resources are helping facilitate their work. These kinds of questions can highlight patterns and lessons relevant across the campus. Senior leaders can also ensure that a record is maintained of efforts across campus so there is a sense of history and movement over time. Additionally, senior-level administrators can set benchmarks for what the institution would like to achieve by certain dates.

At many institutions, provosts and vice provosts work directly with institutional governance bodies (such as university committees of faculty affairs) on policy initiatives and practices related to faculty work. In the context of this work, senior administrators can collaborate with governance leaders to develop institutional policies and plans for periodic review of teaching evaluation practices and establish metrics for establishing new approaches to evaluation. Updating and continually investing in high-quality teaching evaluation is the sort of practice that might be connected to the regular program review cycle.

Senior-level leaders also control some of the institution's financial resources. For example, they may be able to provide funding to support a graduate assistant or a staff person in an institutional research office to establish metrics on department initiatives, collect related data, and synthesize lessons learned. Through their attention to defining metrics, collecting data, and providing the support needed to carry out such work, senior leaders can establish an expectation of continuous improvement.

LEADERSHIP STRATEGY 7: CONNECT TO NATIONAL RESOURCES AND THE NATIONAL DIALOGUE

We have emphasized how plans to transform teaching evaluation need to be appropriate for the institutional context and culture. At the same time, local efforts benefit from connection to national conversations and activity around improving teaching and reforming teaching evaluation. Senior institutional leaders can play a role in supporting those connections. The TEval project has hosted several gatherings of the three participating universities and has cohosted several national meetings of leaders from dozens of institutions engaged in changing teaching evaluation. These convenings have provided venues for discussions of useful strategies, persistent challenges, and emerging lessons around changing teaching evaluation.

In addition to the work in the TEval project, various national initiatives are supporting more learner-focused teaching and more holistic approaches to teaching evaluation, as well as discussions about the changing nature of academic work and careers, broader definitions of "what counts" as faculty work, and the need to improve evaluation processes for all aspects of academic work. Chapter 2 delineated some of these efforts. For example, the National Academies of Sciences, Engineering, and Medicine established a Roundtable on Systemic Change in STEM

Undergraduate Education in 2017. Its mission is to encourage systemic efforts to improve teaching and learning in STEM undergraduate education, to connect projects and initiatives with similar goals, to analyze the changing context of learning in higher education, and to identify issues and gaps still to be addressed in support of deeper STEM undergraduate learning. From 2020 to 2025, the Howard Hughes Medical Institute also supported an ambitious project, Inclusive Excellence 3 (IE3), that brought together university teams to work on improving learning for a diverse body of students. A central goal of this initiative was developing approaches to evaluate effective and inclusive teaching, recognizing that this is fundamental to advancing educational equity.

We mention these national initiatives as examples of the kinds of communities and projects in which universities and colleges may choose to be involved. The interest and commitment of senior institutional leaders—provosts or teaching center directors, for example—is usually necessary for institutional involvement in national projects. Becoming part of national efforts and projects provides opportunities for institutional administrators and faculty members working on teaching evaluation projects to interact with like-minded colleagues. Such interactions have been well-received as opportunities to offer mutual encouragement and discuss successes and challenges, leadership strategies, and useful resources. When a university or college participates in such a project, the opportunity to interact and share ideas with peers at other institutions and the prestige of being part of a funded national initiative can motivate individual faculty members and institutional leaders. We also have observed that institutions connected with national projects can leverage the prestige of the larger initiatives to enhance the visibility and stature of their own campus work.

Connecting institutional work on teaching evaluation to accreditation policies and processes can also motivate faculty members and leaders. Departmental and institutional efforts to develop more holistic and effective teaching evaluation often lead to faculty discussions about intended teaching outcomes. At CU, the history department faculty refined their understanding and articulation of their undergraduate program's student learning outcomes as they worked on revising teaching evaluation. This effort was useful in preparing documents for national accreditation review. A comprehensive approach to teaching evaluation situates a department well for highlighting its contributions to institutional missions and priorities around supporting student success. At the institutional level, provosts and deans can point out the connections between the conversations needed to transform teaching evaluation and the efforts needed to prepare for disciplinary or institutional accreditation review. Shining light on these synergetic connections may encourage faculty to invest their time in transforming teaching evaluation.

Meanwhile, institutional leaders will recognize the increasing public discussion surrounding higher education. In particular, one vein of the public dialogue focuses on questioning the worth and value of higher education. Investing in high-quality educational practices and having the capacity to evaluate our teaching practices in a scholarly way is one mechanism to simultaneously note the public concern and proactively demonstrate our value as a public good. Whether for the public, policymakers, future students, alumni, or donors and funders, our higher education institutions can use high-quality evaluation practices to demonstrate their commitment to our core purpose of educating learners to participate in the workforce and broader society.

IMPORTANT POINTS TO TAKE FROM THIS CHAPTER

Senior-level institutional leaders, including provosts and vice provosts, deans, and directors of teaching centers, are crucial to major change initiatives. Senior leaders are in roles that impact the whole institution, enabling them to support the systemic nature of a major change initiative. While reforming teaching evaluation can start with departmental leaders and certainly depends on the work of administrators and staff at the department level, senior-level leaders are essential to changing teaching evaluation. They can identify and help adapt relevant institutional policies, provide resources to support the change work, connect people across the institution for collaboration, and signal the alignment of the change work with institutional priorities and mission.

This chapter highlights strategies that senior-level institutional leaders can use to advance the transformation of teaching evaluation. We recommend that they be used not as a linear checklist but as a set of complementary, integrated levers for change to be adapted to each particular institutional context. The strategies recommended include:

- Situate efforts to change teaching evaluation in the specific institutional context.
- Recognize and manage the change process over time.
- Motivate faculty to join efforts to transform teaching evaluation.
- Connect and convene key leaders and allies across the institution who can help advance plans to transform teaching evaluation.
- Encourage the creation of resources that support new approaches to teaching evaluation.
- Manage barriers and monitor progress in the process of transforming teaching evaluation.
- Connect to national resources and the national dialogue.

5

Taking the Next Steps

IT IS CLEAR THAT our instructors and institutions need more modern approaches to evaluating teaching. Educational practices are changing, limitations and biases in our current forms of evaluation are clear, and the demographics of students and the roles of educators are shifting. Building on decades of research, we introduce a more robust and adaptable model of teaching evaluation that both develops educators and holds them accountable. It allows for a common campus-wide approach while providing contextualization for different roles and disciplinary foci within the institution; aligns our process with actual teaching practices in a transparent, equitable, and developmental fashion; and connects institutional practices and resources with higher education's core mission—education.

The TEval approach centers on a research-validated framework that defines the dimensions of high-quality teaching practices and frames the forms of data to be collected from three essential sources: students, peers, and the instructor. Chapter 1 explains the TEval framework, and subsequent chapters provide a roadmap for institutions seeking to enact and sustain these more robust approaches. A focus on the department and discipline is essential, and chapter 3 describes how departments can transform and deploy these updated evaluation practices. Such changes must occur as part of a systemic and holistic approach (framed in chapter 2) and must be part of a campus-wide strategy (described in chapter 4). A process of continuous improvement helps sustain changes and keeps them current. In being explicit about our approaches to evaluation and the metrics we use, we externalize our values, which are central to both the word and process of *evaluation*. In this case, the purpose and underlying values of our educational enterprise focus on advancing the learning of the full array of students arriving on our campuses and supporting the capacities of our faculty and institutions to fulfill our core learning mission.

In this final chapter, we explore the implications of transforming teaching evaluation across three dimensions: (1) as an essential lever of change to support quality education, (2) as a call for collective action across institutions of higher education, and (3) as a model for broader shifts in campus culture and approaches to supporting the full span and breadth of faculty practice.

TEACHING EVALUATION AS A LEVER FOR CHANGE IN PRACTICE

An updated, holistic evaluation process is one of the key tools to support effective, inclusive, and equitable teaching practices. It also helps our institutions highlight education as their core mission, especially in an era of significant change and challenges. By establishing a more robust evaluation system, we have the opportunity to clarify, establish, and then put into practice our value system around education. At the heart of "evaluation" is "value": What do we care about? What do we measure? Where do we put resources? To what ends do we develop individually and institutionally? The approaches we present here are applicable whether an institution seeks to develop a breadth of learners equipped to realize a functioning democracy, to focus on certification of the next generation of workers, or any of the other motives for education. They provide tools for individuals, departments, and administrators to align resources and to develop and engage in practices aligned with such a vision.

By enacting *quality* scholarly approaches to teaching evaluation, a campus can address the opportunities and challenges facing higher education. Appropriate teaching evaluations not only promote effective, evidence-based teaching but also can support educational practices that enhance the capacities and diversity of the learners arriving at our institutions. Teaching evaluation is a leading tool in supporting student success.[1] By explicitly focusing evaluation on educational practices that support students, we make visible the kinds of activities and expectations we have for our classrooms and hold those who are responsible for implementing such practices accountable. In parallel, the developmental and transparent approaches to teaching evaluation presented here facilitate and reward the efforts of those very same faculty we are holding accountable; we provide roadmaps for development and recognize the all-too-often hidden labor of high-quality teaching, the work behind the scenes to construct an effective classroom experience, and the educational practices that support learning outside the classroom. Explicitly establishing expectations, providing mechanisms for our faculty to achieve these expectations, and recognizing the breadth of work required to teach effectively will support a more engaged, effective, and professionally valued faculty.

Coupled with the support of students and faculty is the creation of a system that is more equitable, accessible, and inclusive for students and faculty alike. As may be seen at each of the institutions showcased in this volume, on the associated TEval website, and in the departmental case studies on the TEval website, teaching evaluation can be more transparent and developmental and mitigate biases by triangulating among a breadth of data sources.[2] The use of collectively defined frameworks that are turned into rubrics for evaluating faculty establishes common expectations, provides pathways for improvement, and guides how evaluation is to occur. High-quality teaching evaluations build more inclusive and equitable learning environments by seeking to evaluate those outcomes rather than assuming they will be achieved. Appropriate evaluations also support those faculty from diverse backgrounds who often sit at a disadvantage in our educational systems. Appropriate evaluations address the biases and limitations built into the current systems. Meanwhile, explicit and transparent teaching evaluations can also address the symptoms of faculty burnout by focusing on its root causes—increasing workload and overwork.[3] Teaching evaluation can recognize the expanding work that faculty are taking on, allow us to consider what roles instructors should not be taking on, and can be used to explicitly define and enact a humane scale of work. Ultimately, these high-quality practices will advance efforts directed at retention and development of the broad array of participants—both students and faculty—we seek in our institutions.

At the administrative level, high-quality teaching evaluation advances institutional effectiveness and reputation. It also has the potential to improve our institutions' financial health, especially as more institutions rely on tuition dollars (due to systemic public defunding of higher education). In short, improved teaching practices lead to increased engagement and a sense of belonging among students.[4] An increased sense of belonging leads to increased retention.[5] Increased retention leads to increased revenue.[6] While that involves a chain of causal reasoning, current efforts to improve teaching evaluation, such as at the three institutions discussed in this book, seek to strengthen such findings and put them into action by establishing appropriate institutional policies. In parallel, these moves represent an excellent public relations opportunity. High-quality teaching evaluation that leads to improved student learning can effectively message to the public that we in higher education are committed to the core mission of learning—to simultaneously support individuals, a functioning, democratic society, and an economic engine that underpins our society. Ultimately, by investing in individuals' development and learning through high-quality teaching practice, we invest in a democracy of educated and informed citizens (as envisioned in the founding of our country). It also signals to the public that we are holding ourselves accountable for one of society's most essential social, cultural, and democratic practices—education.

COLLECTIVE ACTION TOWARD SYSTEMIC CHANGE IN TEACHING EVALUATION AND BEYOND

If our collective, overarching goal is to scale and accelerate the use of more robust and equitable approaches to teaching evaluation, then we must act across our large and diverse group of institutions, while studying the change process in different institutional contexts. Research has shown that collaborative structures (e.g., networks or alliances) that enable individuals and institutions to work together around shared goals have distinct abilities to scale change.[7] Such collaborative structures foster communities that provide avenues for the development and exchange of ideas about change strategies, offer encouragement to those working to manage barriers or resistance in their home institutions, and provide credibility by creating conversation and rationale at the national level.

Over the last several years, interest and work on more effective approaches to teaching evaluation have grown both nationally and internationally. For instance, the Association of American Universities (AAU) has focused on this issue as part of its STEM Initiative, including funding five STEM department demonstration projects and a broader learning community on teaching evaluation.[8] The Howard Hughes Medical Institute (HHMI) made the evaluation of effective and inclusive teaching a major theme of its Inclusive Excellence 3 initiative, and the National Academies of Sciences, Engineering, and Medicine (NASEM) Roundtable on Systemic Change in Undergraduate STEM Education has focused part of its work on teaching evaluation. This growth in interest enabled the TEval coalition to help shape and propel a national dialogue around transforming teaching evaluation. Those within TEval have collaborated with several other communities, including the AAU, the Association of Public and Land-grant Universities (APLU), the Accelerating System Change Network (ASCN), the Bay View Alliance, HHMI, and the NASEM Roundtable, to bring awareness to this topic and advance collective discussion. This included organizing a workshop at the National Academies in 2019 and a NASEM-sponsored National Dialogue in January 2021.[9] In October 2021, TEval hosted an online, three-day public knowledge exchange for more than 220 people from ninety institutions.

Outcomes of these events included connecting people who were already interested in transforming teaching evaluation, bringing greater attention to the topic, and fostering community- and capacity-building for the work. The campus-level change efforts within TEval and those at other institutions were accelerated through the national dialogue. Building on this momentum, TEval hosted a summit on teaching evaluation in June 2023. It gathered more than forty people from twenty-five colleges and universities as well as six national organizations at the HHMI headquarters. The group coalesced around a vision of building a national coalition of institutions that would broaden awareness of the need to change teaching evaluation and expand and support institutions and individuals working toward this change.

Next steps are underway in continuing these discussions, and any institution invested in transforming its own teaching evaluation efforts is encouraged to partner with others. Simply connecting to like-minded institutions will benefit all involved. Sharing and drawing from the vast and growing body of resources, like those presented in this book, will advance the opportunities for change. The national attention and interest in this subject mean that institutions do not have to create their own paths. In fact, the enthusiasm for this work, breadth of participation, engagement of national-scale organizations, and successes achieved so far are markers of an early-stage movement. Join these efforts as they emerge. Contribute to them and foster their development—for your own institution's sake and for our collective welfare, yes, but also for the learners who benefit from participating in the social enterprise of higher education.

Although action and engagement are needed, such action must be informed by scholarship. We need to expand our knowledge of effective approaches to teaching evaluation and of the ways to select, develop, and embed those approaches. Additionally, since the use of collaborative networks to advance and scale change in higher education is growing, more needs to be understood about how such approaches to improve teaching evaluation can be most effectively initiated, organized, and sustained. Researchers and practitioners of institutional transformation alike can contribute to advance knowledge around at least four key questions:

1) *Approaches to transforming teaching evaluation*: What are effective and equitable models of teaching evaluation, and how do those vary based on institutional characteristics and contexts?
2) *Institutional embedding and scaling*: What are effective institutional strategies for integrating and scaling transformed teaching evaluation practices?
3) *Impact of changing teaching evaluation*: How can teaching evaluation catalyze broader institutional changes that support successful outcomes for our learners?
4) *Cross-institutional scaling*: What characterizes the impact, affordances, and challenges of an alliance approach to scaling and accelerating transformational change?

LEVERAGING THESE APPROACHES TO SUPPORT BROADER CHANGE

Given the radical changes facing higher education, the reform of teaching evaluation may only be the first step in modernizing higher education. The success of educational transformation in our teaching practice can serve as a model for a more holistic update of our overall faculty evaluation systems. That is, teaching evaluation may be seen as a first step in a broader, systemic approach to modernizing and aligning our evaluation systems with institutional practices and operations.

In recent decades, the work of faculty has broadened significantly.[10] In addition to teaching and service work (and, at some institutions, knowledge generation through research), faculty are engaging in a host of new practices or practices that have grown significantly in recent years. These activities include managing new information technologies, addressing issues of student mental health and well-being, managing classroom safety, attending to students' disabilities and accommodations, reporting student outcomes, and documenting and supporting public impact. The same approaches that we take to externalize our values through the process of teaching evaluation can be used as we transform faculty evaluation more broadly. An incremental approach would be to add categories beyond the standard of research, teaching, and service—such as Elrod and colleagues' Scholarship of Mission, which focuses on advancing institutional goals.[11] More radically, one could imagine a day where universities and colleges no longer artificially separate research, teaching, and service categories in faculty work but instead value and honor the breadth of work to which faculty and their institutions are committed. The efforts of many, including the National Academies of Sciences, Engineering, and Medicine, the Association for Undergraduate Education at Research Universities (UERU), and the HuMetricsHSS initiative to create a values-based framework to capture the breadth of work in scholarly life, point to such a future.[12]

In this volume, we have identified approaches that may be useful for such initiatives seeking to go beyond transforming teaching evaluations:

- *Take a systems perspective*: Any effort to foster significant or transformative change in higher education benefits from a systems approach. Understanding both the ecosystem within an institution and the ecosystem in which your institution is a part will identify the actors, programs, and policies needed for considering sustained change.

- *Identify the right unit of change and act "glocally"*:[13] For many research-focused and larger institutions, the department is a critical locus of change. It is at this level that faculty members are hired, policies are established, and change is sustained. These loci of change do not function in a vacuum, though. By acting locally and by recognizing that individual efforts are connected to the broader system, participants in change initiatives can achieve results that are more sustainable and significant. That is, a local effort ensures relevance in a specific context even as it contributes to a global approach, which provides stability, permanence, and commonality across the system of change.
- *Assess readiness to change*: Effective change processes begin with consideration of what strategies will fit the institutional context and attention to the multiple levels of the organization.
- *Select and use multiple synergistic strategies*: Successful transformative change processes use multiple strategies, or levers, for change that recognize and influence the interrelated parts of an institution. An integrated top-down, bottom-up, and middle-out approach involving senior institutional leaders, department-level leaders, and faculty members has the most potential to achieve any major goal. The objective of change should balance a set of prescriptive outcomes (e.g., moving away from and reducing the emphasis on student rating systems) and emergent outcomes (e.g., community-developed standards for evaluation that draw from scholarly frameworks). That is, successful change efforts tend to draw on established, effective approaches and adapt those to local circumstances so that results are locally valid and recognizable.
- *Provide resources and expertise*: Sustained change requires dedicated people, adequate funding, and material and intellectual resources.

Such efforts often begin as voluntary practice, but long-term sustained work must be built into the institutional organization (including funding and reward structures).

- *Communicate and value progress*: Communicating goals and rationale for the work, committing to transparent and inclusive approaches, and valuing, recognizing, and rewarding those conducting the work will contribute to progress. Also, never underestimate the value of celebration and community building. They promote common values, engage those invested in the change process, and ultimately promote the vision driving the transformation.
- *Sustain change and plan for long-term success through continuous improvement*: Change takes time and is supported by establishing benchmarks, monitoring progress, and evaluating achievement of goals. Modest steps, even seemingly small, if organized in the context of a systems approach, will add up to advance a larger goal. Building on these steps through a process of evaluation, reflection, and continuous improvement will support the success of strategic initiatives. Throughout any effort, change leaders should consider what check-ins are necessary to gauge progress, how efforts may adapt to changing contexts and circumstances, and how the effort will respond to the dynamic processes of systemic change.

Of course, the compelling purpose and the bottom line of high-quality educational practice is to support our remarkable learners, advancing their capacities and interests and seeding the future we hope to bring about. Thoughtful and thorough teaching evaluation strongly supports this goal. It engages faculty in clarifying learning outcomes, highlights the centrality of effective teaching practices, recognizes the many approaches to teaching and learning embedded in disciplines and institutions, showcases the full array of work involved in excellent teaching, and upholds learning as a core value and goal of our institutions.

ACKNOWLEDGMENTS

WE APPRECIATE THE INTELLECTUAL support for the work presented in this book from the Bay View Alliance, the Association of American Universities (AAU), the Association of Public and Land-Grant Universities, and the National Academies of Sciences, Engineering, and Medicine and leaders therein who have helped us advance the international dialogue, promoting scholarly teaching evaluation in support of the foundational missions of higher education.

This material is based upon work supported, in part, by the National Science Foundation (NSF), Award numbers: DUE 1725946, 1726087, 1725959, and 1725956. We are grateful for the national leadership that NSF has demonstrated over many decades in the area of ensuring excellence in STEM education. Any opinions, findings, and conclusions or recommendations expressed in this material are those of the authors and do not necessarily reflect the views of the National Science Foundation. We also acknowledge support from the Howard Hughes Medical Institute (HHMI).

We also express appreciation for the contributions to our TEval project made by colleagues Sarah Andrews, Debbie Carlisle, Kaila Colyott, Mark Graham, Cynthia Hampton, Jessica Keating, Dan Bernstein, Aesha Mustafa, and Meagan Patterson. Our thanks also to the many department and faculty partners who led the way for their peers in adapting and incubating the TEval-based approaches and shared their experiences and insights with us.

NOTES

FOREWORD

1. Brenda Vyletel, Erin Voichoski, Sarah Lipson, and Justin Heinze, "Exploring Faculty Burnout Through the 2022–23 HMS Faculty/Staff Survey," American Psychological Association, August 31, 2023, https://www.apa.org/ed/precollege/psychology-teacher-network/introductory-psychology/faculty-burnout-survey.
2. Gallup and Lumina Foundation, *State of Higher Education 2024 Report* (Gallup, 2024), https://www.gallup.com/analytics/644939/state-of-higher-education.aspx.
3. Bernhard G. Gunter, "Fix It—Don't Throw It Out: Student Evaluations of Teaching Are Valuable, but the System Needs Reform," *Liberal Education* 110, no. 4 (2024): https://www.aacu.org/liberaleducation/articles/fix-it-dont-throw-it-out.

INTRODUCTION

1. Ernest Boyer, *Scholarship Reconsidered: Priorities of the Professoriate* (Carnegie Foundation for the Advancement of Teaching, 1990); Boyer 2030 Commission, "The Equity-Excellence Imperative: A 2030 Blueprint for Undergraduate Education at U.S. Research Universities" (Association for Undergraduate Education at Research Universities [UERU], 2022); Boyer Commission on Educating Undergraduates in the Research University, "Reinventing Undergraduate Education: A Blueprint for America's Research Universities" (Stony Brook University, 1998); Pat Hutchings, Mary T. Huber, and Anthony Ciccone, *The Scholarship of Teaching and Learning Reconsidered: Institutional Integration and Impact* (Jossey-Bass/Wiley, 2011).
2. National Science Board, National Science Foundation, "Science and Engineering Indicators 2022: The State of U.S. Science and Engineering," 2022, https://ncses.nsf.gov/pubs/nsb20221; Wolfgang Stroebe, "Student Evaluations of Teaching Encourages Poor Teaching and Contributes to Grade Inflation: A

Theoretical and Empirical Analysis," *Basic and Applied Social Psychology* 42, no. 4 (July 3, 2020): 276–94, https://doi.org/10.1080/01973533.2020.1756817; Adrianna J. Kezar, ed., *Embracing Non-Tenure Track Faculty: Changing Campuses for the New Faculty Majority* (Routledge, 2012); Mark Lee et al., "An Instructional-Workforce Framework for Coordinated Change in Undergraduate Education," *Change: The Magazine of Higher Learning* 55, no. 1 (January 2, 2023): 54–63, https://doi.org/10.1080/00091383.2023.2151809.

3. Maura Borrego and Charles Henderson, "Increasing the Use of Evidence-Based Teaching in STEM Higher Education: A Comparison of Eight Change Strategies," *Journal of Engineering Education* 103, no. 2 (April 2014): 220–52, https://doi.org/10.1002/jee.20040; Dee L. Fink, *Creating Significant Learning Experiences: An Integrated Approach to Designing College Courses* (Wiley, 2013); Marsha C. Lovett, *How Learning Works: Eight Research-Based Principles for Smart Teaching*, 2nd ed. (Wiley, 2023).
4. Neil Hatfield, Nathanial Brown, and Chad M. Topaz, "Do Introductory Courses Disproportionately Drive Minoritized Students out of STEM Pathways?," ed. Michele Gelfand, *PNAS Nexus* 1, no. 4 (September 1, 2022): pgac167, https://doi.org/10.1093/pnasnexus/pgac167; National Academies of Sciences, Engineering, and Medicine, *Transforming Undergraduate STEM Education: Supporting Equitable and Effective Teaching* (National Academies Press, 2025); National Science Board, National Science Foundation, "Science and Engineering Indicators 2022"; M. Stains et al., "Anatomy of STEM Teaching in North American Universities," *Science* 359, no. 6383 (March 30, 2018): 1468–70, https://doi.org/10.1126/science.aap8892.
5. Adrienne Lu, "Faculty and Staff Are Feeling Anxious, Depressed, and Burnt Out, Study Says," *Chronicle of Higher Education*, December 3, 2024, https://www.chronicle.com/article/faculty-and-staff-are-feeling-anxious-depressed-and-burnt-out-study-says.
6. Michael Dennin et al., "Aligning Practice to Policies: Changing the Culture to Recognize and Reward Teaching at Research Universities" (Association of American Universities/Research Corporation for Scientific Advancement, December 2017), https://www.aau.edu/sites/default/files/AAU-Files/STEM-Education-Initiative/Aligning-Practice-To-Policies-Digital.pdf; Michael Dennin et al., "Aligning Practice to Policies: Changing the Culture to Recognize and Reward Teaching at Research Universities," ed. C. Gary Reiness, *CBE—Life Sciences Education* 16, no. 4 (December 2017): es5, https://doi.org/10.1187/cbe.17-02-0032; Gabriela C. Weaver et al., "Establishing a Better Approach for Evaluating Teaching: The TEval Project," *Change: The Magazine of Higher Learning* 52, no. 3 (May 3, 2020): 25–31, https://doi.org/10.1080/00091383.2020.1745575.
7. Dennin et al., "Aligning Practice to Policies"; Dennin et al., "Aligning Practice to Policies"; National Academies of Sciences, Engineering, and Medicine,

"Recognizing and Evaluating Teaching in Higher Education: Proceedings of a Workshop in Brief," 2020, http://nap.edu/25685.

8. Stroebe, "Student Evaluations of Teaching"; Bob Uttl, Carmela A. White, and Daniela Wong Gonzalez, "Meta-Analysis of Faculty's Teaching Effectiveness: Student Evaluation of Teaching Ratings and Student Learning Are Not Related," *Studies in Educational Evaluation* 54 (September 2017): 22–42, https://doi.org/10.1016/j.stueduc.2016.08.007.
9. Rosemary Fisher, Chamila Perera, and Richard Laferriere, "Unintended Consequences: When Innovation in Pedagogy Impacts Student Evaluations," *International Journal of Changes in Education* 1, no. 4 (November 15, 2024): 169–76, https://doi.org/10.47852/bonviewIJCE42023045.
10. Yesim Capa-Aydin, "Student Evaluation of Instruction: Comparison Between In-Class and Online Methods," *Assessment & Evaluation in Higher Education* 41, no. 1 (January 2, 2016): 112–26, https://doi.org/10.1080/02602938.2014.987106.
11. Daniel S. Hamermesh and Amy Parker, "Beauty in the Classroom: Instructors' Pulchritude and Putative Pedagogical Productivity," *Economics of Education Review* 24, no. 4 (August 2005): 369–76, https://doi.org/10.1016/j.econedurev.2004.07.013; Michael A. McPherson and R. Todd Jewell, "Leveling the Playing Field: Should Student Evaluation Scores Be Adjusted?," *Social Science Quarterly* 88, no. 3 (September 2007): 868–81, https://doi.org/10.1111/j.1540-6237.2007.00487.x; B. P. Smith, "Student Ratings of Teacher Effectiveness: An Analysis of End-of-Course Faculty Evaluation," *College Student Journal* 41 (n.d.): 788–800.
12. Hamermesh and Parker, "Beauty in the Classroom"; Friederike Mengel, Jan Sauermann, and Ulf Zölitz, "Gender Bias in Teaching Evaluations," *Journal of the European Economic Association* 17, no. 2 (April 1, 2019): 535–66, https://doi.org/10.1093/jeea/jvx057; Stroebe, "Student Evaluations of Teaching."
13. Kezar, *Embracing Non-Tenure Track Faculty*; Lee et al., "An Instructional-Workforce Framework."
14. Daniel J. Bernstein, "Peer Review and Evaluation of the Intellectual Work of Teaching," *Change: The Magazine of Higher Learning* 40, no. 2 (March 2008): 48–51, https://doi.org/10.3200/CHNG.40.2.48-51; Charles E. Glassick, Mary T. Huber, and Gene I. Maeroff, *Scholarship Assessed: Evaluation of the Professoriate*, A Special Report (Jossey-Bass, 1997); Pat Hutchings, *From Idea to Prototype: The Peer Review of Teaching: A Project Workbook* (AAHE Teaching Initiative, American Association for Higher Education, 1995); Pat Hutchings, *Making Teaching Community Property: A Menu for Peer Collaboration and Peer Review* (Taylor & Francis, 1996); Hutchings, Huber, and Ciccone, *The Scholarship of Teaching and Learning Reconsidered*; Adrian Renea Lyde, David C. Grieshaber, and George Byrns, "Faculty Teaching Performance: Perceptions of a Multi-Source Method for Evaluation," *Journal of the Scholarship of Teaching and Learning* 16, no. 3 (June 17, 2016): 82–94, https://doi.org/10.14434/josotl.v16i3.18145.

15. Andrea Follmer Greenhoot, Doug Ward, and Dan B. Bernstein, "Benchmarks for Teaching Effectiveness" (KU Center for Teaching Excellence, 2017), https://cte.ku.edu/benchmarks-teaching-effectiveness; Andrea Follmer Greenhoot et al., "Benchmarks for Teaching Effectiveness" (KU Center for Teaching Excellence, 2020), https://cte.ku.edu/benchmarks-teaching-effectiveness; Andrea Follmer Greenhoot et al., "Benchmarks for Teaching Effectiveness" (KU Center for Teaching Excellence, 2024), https://cte.ku.edu/benchmarks-teaching-effectiveness.
16. Justin Esarey and Natalie Valdes, "Unbiased, Reliable, and Valid Student Evaluations Can Still Be Unfair," *Assessment & Evaluation in Higher Education* 45, no. 8 (November 16, 2020): 1106–20, https://doi.org/10.1080/02602938.2020.1724875.
17. Anthony S. Bryk et al., *Learning to Improve: How America's Schools Can Get Better at Getting Better* (Harvard Education Press, 2015).
18. John Tagg, "Why Does the Faculty Resist Change?," *Change: The Magazine of Higher Learning* 44, no. 1 (January 4, 2012): 6–15, https://doi.org/10.1080/00091383.2012.635987.
19. Peter D. Eckel and Adrianna Kezar, "Key Strategies for Making New Institutional Sense: Ingredients to Higher Education Transformation," *Higher Education Policy* 16, no. 1 (March 2003): 39–53, https://doi.org/10.1057/palgrave.hep.8300001; Adrianna Kezar, "Understanding Sensemaking/Sensegiving in Transformational Change Processes from the Bottom Up," *Higher Education* 65, no. 6 (June 2013): 761–80, https://doi.org/10.1007/s10734-012-9575-7; Adrianna J. Kezar, *How Colleges Change: Understanding, Leading, and Enacting Change*, 2nd ed. (Routledge, Taylor & Francis, 2018).
20. "TEval: Transforming Higher Education—Multidimensional Evaluation of Teaching," TEval (website), n.d., https://TEval.net/.
21. Sandhya Krishnan et al., "Guides to Advance Teaching Evaluation (GATEs): A Resource for STEM Departments Planning Robust and Equitable Evaluation Practices," ed. Cynthia Bauerle, *CBE—Life Sciences Education* 21, no. 3 (September 2022): ar42, https://doi.org/10.1187/cbe.21-08-0198; Stephanie Salomone et al., "Making Teaching Matter More: REFLECT at the University of Portland," in *Transforming Institutions: Accelerating Systemic Change in Higher Education*, ed. Kate White et al. (Pressbooks, 2020), https://openbooks.library.umass.edu/ascnti2020/; Shawn R. Simonson, Brittnee Earl, and Megan Frary, "Establishing a Framework for Assessing Teaching Effectiveness," *College Teaching* 70, no. 2 (April 3, 2022): 164–80, https://doi.org/10.1080/87567555.2021.1909528; Glory Tobiason and Adrienne Lavine, "Holistic Evaluation of Teaching" (UCLA Center for the Advancement of Teaching, 2022), https://teaching.ucla.edu/holistic-evaluation-of-teaching/.
22. Andrea Follmer Greenhoot et al., "Variations on Embedded Expert Models: Implementing Change Initiatives That Support Departments from Within," in

Transforming Institutions: Accelerating Systemic Change in Higher Education, ed. Kate White et al. (Pressbooks, 2020), https://openbooks.library.umass.edu/ascnti2020/; Carl E. Wieman, *Improving How Universities Teach Science: Lessons from the Science Education Initiative* (Harvard University Press, 2017).

CHAPTER 1

1. Daniel J. Bernstein, "Peer Review and Evaluation of the Intellectual Work of Teaching," *Change: The Magazine of Higher Learning* 40, no. 2 (March 2008): 48–51, https://doi.org/10.3200/CHNG.40.2.48-51; Dan Bernstein and Mary T. Huber, "What Is Good Teaching? Raising the Bar Through Scholarship Assessed" (International Society for the Scholarship of Teaching and Learning, 2006); Charles E. Glassick, Mary T. Huber, and Gene I. Maeroff, *Scholarship Assessed: Evaluation of the Professoriate*, A Special Report (Jossey-Bass, 1997); Pat Hutchings, *From Idea to Prototype: The Peer Review of Teaching: A Project Workbook* (AAHE Teaching Initiative, American Association for Higher Education, 1995); Pat Hutchings, *Making Teaching Community Property: A Menu for Peer Collaboration and Peer Review* (Taylor & Francis, 1996); Adrian Renea Lyde, David C. Grieshaber, and George Byrns, "Faculty Teaching Performance: Perceptions of a Multi-Source Method for Evaluation," *Journal of the Scholarship of Teaching and Learning* 16, no. 3 (June 17, 2016): 82–94, https://doi.org/10.14434/josotl.v16i3.18145.
2. Michael Dennin et al., *Aligning Practice to Policies: Changing the Culture to Recognize and Reward Teaching at Research Universities* (Association of American Universities/Research Corporation for Scientific Advancement, December 2017), https://www.aau.edu/sites/default/files/AAU-Files/STEM-Education-Initiative/Aligning-Practice-To-Policies-Digital.pdf; Michael Dennin et al., "Aligning Practice to Policies: Changing the Culture to Recognize and Reward Teaching at Research Universities," ed. C. Gary Reiness, *CBE—Life Sciences Education* 16, no. 4 (December 2017): es5, https://doi.org/10.1187/cbe.17-02-0032; National Academies of Sciences, Engineering, and Medicine, *Transforming Undergraduate STEM Education: Supporting Equitable and Effective Teaching* (National Academies Press, 2025).
3. National Academies of Sciences, Engineering, and Medicine, *Transforming Undergraduate STEM Education*; Boyer 2030 Commission, "The Equity-Excellence Imperative: A 2030 Blueprint for Undergraduate Education at U.S. Research Universities" (Association for Undergraduate Education at Research Universities [UERU], 2022).
4. Michelle K. Smith et al., "The Classroom Observation Protocol for Undergraduate STEM (COPUS): A New Instrument to Characterize University STEM Classroom Practices," ed. Erin L. Dolan, *CBE—Life Sciences Education* 12, no. 4 (December 2013): 618–27, https://doi.org/10.1187/cbe.13-08-0154; Michael Piburn and Daiyo Sawada, "Reformed Teaching Observation Protocol (RTOP):

Reference Manual" (Arizona Collaborative for Excellence in the Preparation of Teachers, 2000); Tracie M. Addy et al., "The Development of the Protocol for Advancing Inclusive Teaching Efforts (PAITE)," *Journal of Educational Research and Practice* 12, no. 0 (February 28, 2023), https://doi.org/10.5590/JERAP.2022.12.0.05.

5. Roland Robertson, "Glocalization: Time-Space and Homogeneity-Heterogeneity," in *Global Modernities,* by Mike Featherstone, Scott Lash, and Roland Robertson (SAGE, 1995), 25–44, https://doi.org/10.4135/9781446250563.n2; Fay Patel and Hayley M. Lynch, "Glocalization as an Alternative to Internationalization in Higher Education: Embedding Positive Glocal Learning Perspectives," *International Journal of Teaching and Learning in Higher Education* 25 (2013): 223–30.

CHAPTER 2

1. Ann Austin, "Promoting Evidence-Based Change in Undergraduate Science Education" (National Academies: Board on Science Education of the National Academies National Research Council, 2011); Adrianna J. Kezar, *How Colleges Change: Understanding, Leading, and Enacting Change,* 2nd ed. (Routledge, Taylor & Francis, 2018).
2. Austin, "Promoting Evidence-Based Change in Undergraduate Science Education"; Kezar, *How Colleges Change*; Peter Plastrik, *Connecting to Change the World: Harnessing the Power of Networks for Social Impact* (Island, 2014); Jon McPhedran Waitzer and Roshan Paul, "Scaling Social Impact: When Everybody Contributes, Everybody Wins," *Innovations: Technology, Governance, Globalization* 6, no. 2 (April 2011): 143–55, https://doi.org/10.1162/INOV_a_00074.
3. Kezar, *How Colleges Change.*
4. C. Argyris, "How Learning and Reasoning Processes Affect Organizational Change," in *Change in Organizations,* ed. P. S. Goodman (Jossey-Bass, 1982); C. Argyris, *On Organizational Learning* (Blackwell, 1994); Donald A. Schön, *The Reflective Practitioner: How Professionals Think in Action* (Basic Books, 1983).
5. Argyris, "How Learning and Reasoning Processes Affect Organizational Change"; Argyris, *On Organizational Learning.*
6. Kezar, *How Colleges Change,* 63.
7. John P. Kotter, *Leading Change* (Harvard Business School Press, 1996); John P. Kotter, *The Leadership Factor* (Free Press; Collier Macmillan, 1988); John P. Kotter, *Power and Influence* (Free Press, 1985).
8. Kim Cameron and John C. Smart, "Maintaining Effectiveness Amid Downsizing and Decline in Institutions of Higher Education," *Research in Higher Education* 1 (1998): 65–86.
9. Argyris, "How Learning and Reasoning Processes Affect Organizational Change"; Argyris, *On Organizational Learning*; Kezar, *How Colleges Change*; Gareth Morgan, *Images of Organization,* updated ed. (Sage, 2006); Schön, *The*

Reflective Practitioner; Karl E. Weick, *Sensemaking in Organizations*, Foundations for Organizational Science (Sage, 1995).

10. Lee Bolman and Terrence Deal, *Reframing Organizations*, 6th ed. (Jossey-Bass, 2017); K. S. Cameron, "Organizational Adaptation and Higher Education," in *Organization and Governance in Higher Education*, 4th ed., ed. M. W. Peterson, E. E. Chaffe, and T. H. White (Ginn, 1991); Kenneth Shaw and Kathryn Lee, "Effecting Change at Syracuse University: The Importance of Values, Mission, and Vision," *Metropolitan Universities: An International Forum* 7, no. 4 (1997): 23–30; Edgar H. Schein, *Organizational Culture and Leadership*, 3rd ed., Jossey-Bass Business & Management Series (Jossey-Bass, 2004).
11. Adrianna Kezar and Peter Eckel, "Examining the Institutional Transformation Process: The Importance of Sensemaking, Inter-Related Strategies and Balance," *Research in Higher Education* 43, no. 3 (2002): 295–328, https://doi.org/10.1023/A:1014889001242.
12. Bolman and Deal, *Reframing Organizations*; Patricia J. Gumport, "The Contested Terrain of Academic Program Reduction," *Journal of Higher Education* 64 (1993): 283–311; Kezar, *How Colleges Change*; Gary Rhoades, "Rethinking Restructuring in Universities," *Journal for Higher Education Management* 10, no. 2 (1995): 17–30.
13. Robert Birnbaum, *How Colleges Work: The Cybernetics of Academic Organization and Leadership*, Jossey-Bass Higher Education Series (Jossey-Bass, 1988); Cameron, "Organizational Adaptation and Higher Education"; Kezar, *How Colleges Change*; Morgan, *Images of Organization*.
14. Kezar, *How Colleges Change*; Walter W. Powell and Paul DiMaggio, eds., *The New Institutionalism in Organizational Analysis* (University of Chicago Press, 1991); Gary Rhoades and Sheila Slaughter, "Academic Capitalism, Managed Professionals, and Supply-Side Higher Education," *Social Text*, no. 51 (1997): 9, https://doi.org/10.2307/466645; Sheila Slaughter and Gary Rhoades, *Academic Capitalism and the New Economy: Markets, State, and Higher Education* (Johns Hopkins University Press, 2004).
15. Mary E. Boyce, "Organizational Learning Is Essential to Achieving and Sustaining Change in Higher Education," *Innovative Higher Education* 28, no. 2 (2003): 119–36, https://doi.org/10.1023/B:IHIE.0000006287.69207.00; Kezar, *How Colleges Change*.
16. Bolman and Deal, *Reframing Organizations*.
17. Sandra Laursen and Ann E. Austin, *Building Gender Equity in the Academy: Institutional Strategies for Change* (Johns Hopkins University Press, 2020); Daniel L. Reinholz and Naneh Apkarian, "Four Frames for Systemic Change in STEM Departments," *International Journal of STEM Education* 5, no. 1 (December 2018): 3, https://doi.org/10.1186/s40594-018-0103-x.
18. Association of American Universities (AAU), "Framework for Systemic Change in Undergraduate STEM Education," AAU, 2013, accessed August 27, 2024, https://osf.io/preprints/osf/q6u2x; Emily R. Miller et al., "Catalyzing

Institutional Transformation: Insights from the AAU STEM Initiative," *Change: The Magazine of Higher Learning* 49, no. 5 (September 3, 2017): 36–45, https://doi.org/10.1080/00091383.2017.1366810.

19. Mark Lee et al., "An Instructional-Workforce Framework for Coordinated Change in Undergraduate Education," *Change: The Magazine of Higher Learning* 55, no. 1 (January 2, 2023): 54–63, https://doi.org/10.1080/00091383.2023.2151809.
20. Susan Elrod and Adrianna Kezar, "Increasing Student Success in STEM: Summary of a Guide to Systemic Institutional Change," *Change: The Magazine of Higher Learning* 49, no. 4 (July 4, 2017): 26–34, https://doi.org/10.1080/00091383.2017.1357097; Susan Elrod et al., eds., "Increasing Student Success in STEM: An Overview for a New Guide to Systemic Institutional Change," in *Transforming Institutions: Undergraduate STEM Education for the 21st Century* (Purdue University Press, 2016), 67–74.
21. Laursen and Austin, *Building Gender Equity in the Academy*; Sandra L. Laursen et al., "ADVANCing the Agenda for Gender Equity," *Change: The Magazine of Higher Learning* 47, no. 4 (July 4, 2015): 16–24, https://doi.org/10.1080/00091383.2015.1053767.
22. Laursen and Austin, *Building Gender Equity in the Academy.*
23. Charles Henderson, Andrea Beach, and Noah Finkelstein, "Facilitating Change in Undergraduate STEM Instructional Practices: An Analytic Review of the Literature," *Journal of Research in Science Teaching* 48, no. 8 (October 2011): 952–84, https://doi.org/10.1002/tea.20439.
24. Susan Elrod et al., "Change Leadership Toolkit 2.0: A Guide for Advancing Systemic Change in Higher Education," Pullias Center for Higher Education, University of Southern California, 2024, https://pullias.usc.edu/download/change-leadership-toolkit-a-guide-for-advancing-systemic-change-in-higher-education/.
25. Adrianna Kezar et al., "Shared Equity Leadership: Making Equity Everyone's Work" (American Council on Education: University of Southern California, Pullias Center for Higher Education, 2021).
26. Kezar, *How Colleges Change*; J. Douglas Toma, *Building Organizational Capacity: Strategic Management in Higher Education* (Johns Hopkins University Press, 2010).
27. Toma, *Building Organizational Capacity.*
28. Kezar, *How Colleges Change*; Laursen and Austin, *Building Gender Equity in the Academy*; Schein, *Organizational Culture and Leadership*; William G. Tierney, "Organizational Culture in Higher Education: Defining the Essentials," *Journal of Higher Education* 59, no. 1 (January 1988): 2, https://doi.org/10.2307/1981868.
29. Kezar, *How Colleges Change*; Reinholz and Apkarian, "Four Frames for Systemic Change in STEM Departments"; Daniel L. Reinholz et al., "Transforming Undergraduate Education from the Middle Out with Departmental Action

Teams," *Change: The Magazine of Higher Learning* 51, no. 5 (September 3, 2019): 64–70, https://doi.org/10.1080/00091383.2019.1652078.

30. Peter T. Knight and Paul R. Trowler, "Department-Level Cultures and the Improvement of Learning and Teaching," *Studies in Higher Education* 25, no. 1 (March 2000): 69–83, https://doi.org/10.1080/030750700116028; Torgny Roxå and Katarina Mårtensson, "Microcultures and Informal Learning: A Heuristic Guiding Analysis of Conditions for Informal Learning in Local Higher Education Workplaces," *International Journal for Academic Development* 20, no. 2 (April 3, 2015): 193–205, https://doi.org/10.1080/1360144X.2015.1029929; John Tagg, "Why Does the Faculty Resist Change?," *Change: The Magazine of Higher Learning* 44, no. 1 (January 4, 2012): 6–15, https://doi.org/10.1080/00091383.2012.635987.
31. Henderson, Beach, and Finkelstein, "Facilitating Change in Undergraduate STEM Instructional Practices"; Adrianna J. Kezar and Elizabeth M. Holcombe, "Leveraging Multiple Theories of Change to Promote Reform: An Examination of the AAU STEM Initiative," *Educational Policy* 35, no. 6 (September 2021): 985–1013, https://doi.org/10.1177/0895904819843594; Laursen and Austin, *Building Gender Equity in the Academy*.
32. Bolman and Deal, *Reframing Organizations*; Laursen and Austin, *Building Gender Equity in the Academy*; Reinholz and Apkarian, "Four Frames for Systemic Change in STEM Departments."
33. Kezar and Eckel, "Examining the Institutional Transformation Process"; Peter D. Eckel and Adrianna Kezar, "Key Strategies for Making New Institutional Sense: Ingredients to Higher Education Transformation," *Higher Education Policy* 16, no. 1 (March 2003): 39–53, https://doi.org/10.1057/palgrave.hep.8300001; Peter Eckel and Adrianna Kezar, *Taking the Reins: Institutional Transformation in Higher Education* (Rowman & Littlefield/Amer Council Ed, 2011); Kezar, *How Colleges Change*.
34. Eckel and Kezar, "Key Strategies for Making New Institutional Sense"; Kezar, *How Colleges Change*; Kezar and Eckel, "Examining the Institutional Transformation Process."
35. Milton D. Cox, "Introduction to Faculty Learning Communities," *New Directions for Teaching and Learning* 2004, no. 97 (March 2004): 5–23, https://doi.org/10.1002/tl.129; Kristin N. Rainville, Cynthia G. Desrochers, and David G. Title, eds., *Faculty Learning Communities: Communities of Practice That Support, Inspire, Engage and Transform Higher Education Classrooms*, Transforming Teaching and Learning in Higher Education (Information Age, 2024); Sean Gehrke and Adrianna Kezar, "The Roles of STEM Faculty Communities of Practice in Institutional and Departmental Reform in Higher Education," *American Educational Research Journal* 54, no. 5 (October 1, 2017): 803–33, https://doi.org/10.3102/0002831217706736; Adrianna Kezar and Sean Gehrke,

"Communities of Transformation and Their Work Scaling STEM Reform" (University of Southern California, Pullias Center for Higher Education, 2015).

36. Henderson, Beach, and Finkelstein, "Facilitating Change in Undergraduate STEM Instructional Practices"; Laursen and Austin, *Building Gender Equity in the Academy*; Tierney, "Organizational Culture in Higher Education."
37. Bolman and Deal, *Reframing Organizations*; Laursen and Austin, *Building Gender Equity in the Academy*.
38. Kezar, *How Colleges Change*.
39. Barbara K. Curry, *Instituting Enduring Innovations: Achieving Continuity of Change in Higher Education*, ASHE-ERIC Higher Education Report, 1992, 7 (George Washington University, School of Education and Human Development, 1992); Kezar, *How Colleges Change*; Kotter, *The Leadership Factor*.
40. Peter Drucker, *The Price of Management* (Harper and Row, 1954).
41. Kotter, *Leading Change*.
42. Donald M. Berwick, "The Science of Improvement," *JAMA* 299, no. 10 (March 12, 2008): 1182, https://doi.org/10.1001/jama.299.10.1182.
43. Anthony S. Bryk et al., *Learning to Improve: How America's Schools Can Get Better at Getting Better* (Harvard Education Press, 2015).
44. Kezar, *How Colleges Change*; Morgan, *Images of Organization*; Schein, *Organizational Culture and Leadership*.
45. Bolman and Deal, *Reframing Organizations*; Schein, *Organizational Culture and Leadership*.
46. Bryk et al., *Learning to Improve*; W. Gary Martin and Howard Gobstein, "Generating a Networked Improvement Community to Improve Secondary Mathematics Teacher Preparation: Network Leadership, Organization, and Operation," *Journal of Teacher Education* 66, no. 5 (November 2015): 482–93, https://doi.org/10.1177/0022487115602312.
47. John Kania and Mark Kramer, "Collective Impact," *Stanford Social Innovation Review* 9, no. 1 (2011): 36–41.
48. Laursen and Austin, *Building Gender Equity in the Academy*.

CHAPTER 3

1. Peter T. Knight and Paul R. Trowler, "Department-Level Cultures and the Improvement of Learning and Teaching," *Studies in Higher Education* 25, no. 1 (March 1, 2000): 69–83, https://doi.org/10.1080/030750700116028; Torgny Roxå and Katarina Mårtensson, "Microcultures and Informal Learning: A Heuristic Guiding Analysis of Conditions for Informal Learning in Local Higher Education Workplaces," *International Journal for Academic Development* 20, no. 2 (April 3, 2015): 193–205, https://doi.org/10.1080/1360144X.2015.1029929; John Tagg, "Why Does the Faculty Resist Change?," *Change: The Magazine of Higher Learning* 44, no. 1 (January 4, 2012): 6–15, https://doi.org/10.1080/00091383.2012.635987.

2. Andrea Follmer Greenhoot, Doug Ward, and Dan B. Bernstein, "Benchmarks for Teaching Effectiveness" (KU Center for Teaching Excellence, 2017), https://cte.ku.edu/benchmarks-teaching-effectiveness; Andrea Follmer Greenhoot et al., "Benchmarks for Teaching Effectiveness" (KU Center for Teaching Excellence, 2020), https://cte.ku.edu/benchmarks-teaching-effectiveness; Andrea Follmer Greenhoot et al., "Benchmarks for Teaching Effectiveness" (KU Center for Teaching Excellence, 2024), https://cte.ku.edu/benchmarks-teaching-effectiveness.
3. Peter D. Eckel and Adrianna Kezar, "Key Strategies for Making New Institutional Sense: Ingredients to Higher Education Transformation," *Higher Education Policy* 16, no. 1 (March 2003): 39–53, https://doi.org/10.1057/palgrave.hep.8300001; Adrianna Kezar and Peter Eckel, "Examining the Institutional Transformation Process: The Importance of Sensemaking, Inter-Related Strategies and Balance," *Research in Higher Education* 43, no. 3 (2002): 295–328, https://doi.org/10.1023/A:1014889001242; Peter Eckel and Adrianna Kezar, *Taking the Reins: Institutional Transformation in Higher Education* (Rowman & Littlefield/Amer Council Ed, 2011); Adrianna J. Kezar, *How Colleges Change: Understanding, Leading, and Enacting Change*, 2nd ed. (Routledge, Taylor & Francis, 2018); Donald M. Berwick, "The Science of Improvement," *JAMA* 299, no. 10 (March 12, 2008): 1182, https://doi.org/10.1001/jama.299.10.1182; Anthony S. Bryk et al., *Learning to Improve: How America's Schools Can Get Better at Getting Better* (Harvard Education Press, 2015).
4. Kezar, *How Colleges Change*; Daniel L. Reinholz et al., "Transforming Undergraduate Education from the Middle Out with Departmental Action Teams," *Change: The Magazine of Higher Learning* 51, no. 5 (September 3, 2019): 64–70, https://doi.org/10.1080/00091383.2019.1652078.
5. Natalie Mendoza, Phoebe S. K. Young, and Paul S. Sutter, "The History Teaching & Learning Project: Laying the Groundwork for Departmental Change at the University of Colorado Boulder," *Journal of American History* 110, no. 4 (March 1, 2024): 718–28, https://doi.org/10.1093/jahist/jaad354.
6. Mary Taylor Huber and Pat Hutchings, "Dynamics of Departmental Change: Lessons from a Successful STEM Teaching Initiative," *Change: The Magazine of Higher Learning* 53, no. 5 (August 16, 2021): 41–47, https://doi.org/10.1080/00091383.2021.1963154.
7. Susan Elrod and Adrianna Kezar, "Increasing Student Success in STEM: Summary of a Guide to Systemic Institutional Change," *Change: The Magazine of Higher Learning* 49, no. 4 (July 4, 2017): 26–34, https://doi.org/10.1080/00091383.2017.1357097; Sarah Andrews et al., "Transforming Teaching Evaluation in Disciplines: A Model and Case Study of Departmental Change," in *Transforming Institutions: Accelerating Systemic Change in Higher Education*, ed. Kate White et al. (Pressbooks, 2020), https://openbooks.library.umass.edu/ascnti2020/.
8. Michelle K. Smith et al., "The Classroom Observation Protocol for Undergraduate STEM (COPUS): A New Instrument to Characterize University STEM

Classroom Practices," ed. Erin L. Dolan, *CBE—Life Sciences Education* 12, no. 4 (December 2013): 618–27, https://doi.org/10.1187/cbe.13-08-0154.

9. Mark Lee et al., "An Instructional-Workforce Framework for Coordinated Change in Undergraduate Education," *Change: The Magazine of Higher Learning* 55, no. 1 (January 2, 2023): 54–63, https://doi.org/10.1080/00091383.2023.2151809.
10. Lee Bolman and Terrence Deal, *Reframing Organizations*, 6th ed. (Jossey-Bass, 2017).
11. Michael Dennin et al., "Aligning Practice to Policies: Changing the Culture to Recognize and Reward Teaching at Research Universities" (Association of American Universities/Research Corporation for Scientific Advancement, December 2017), https://www.aau.edu/sites/default/files/AAU-Files/STEM-Education-Initiative/Aligning-Practice-To-Policies-Digital.pdf; Michael Dennin et al., "Aligning Practice to Policies: Changing the Culture to Recognize and Reward Teaching at Research Universities," ed. C. Gary Reiness, *CBE—Life Sciences Education* 16, no. 4 (December 2017): es5, https://doi.org/10.1187/cbe.17-02-0032; National Academies of Sciences, Engineering, and Medicine, "Recognizing and Evaluating Teaching in Higher Education: Proceedings of a Workshop in Brief," 2020, http://nap.edu/25685.
12. Berwick, "The Science of Improvement"; Bryk et al., *Learning to Improve*; Eckel and Kezar, "Key Strategies for Making New Institutional Sense"; Eckel and Kezar, *Taking the Reins*; Kezar, *How Colleges Change*; Adrianna Kezar, "Understanding Sensemaking/Sensegiving in Transformational Change Processes from the Bottom Up," *Higher Education* 65, no. 6 (June 2013): 761–80, https://doi.org/10.1007/s10734-012-9575-7; Kezar and Eckel, "Examining the Institutional Transformation Process."
13. Berwick, "The Science of Improvement"; Bryk et al., *Learning to Improve*.
14. Charles Henderson, Andrea Beach, and Noah Finkelstein, "Facilitating Change in Undergraduate STEM Instructional Practices: An Analytic Review of the Literature," *Journal of Research in Science Teaching* 48, no. 8 (October 2011): 952–84, https://doi.org/10.1002/tea.20439; Bolman and Deal, *Reframing Organizations*.
15. Berwick, "The Science of Improvement"; Kezar, "Understanding Sensemaking/Sensegiving in Transformational Change Processes from the Bottom Up"; Kezar, *How Colleges Change*.

CHAPTER 5

1. Boyer 2030 Commission, "The Equity-Excellence Imperative: A 2030 Blueprint for Undergraduate Education at U.S. Research Universities" (Association for Undergraduate Education at Research Universities [UERU], 2022).
2. "TEval: Transforming Higher Education—Multidimensional Evaluation of Teaching," TEval (website), n.d., https://TEval.net/.

3. Zaynab Sabagh, Nathan C. Hall, and Alenoush Saroyan, "Antecedents, Correlates and Consequences of Faculty Burnout," *Educational Research* 60, no. 2 (April 3, 2018): 131–56, https://doi.org/10.1080/00131881.2018.1461573.
4. Karyn L. Lewis et al., "Fitting In or Opting Out: A Review of Key Social-Psychological Factors Influencing a Sense of Belonging for Women in Physics," *Physical Review Physics Education Research* 12, no. 2 (August 1, 2016): 020110, https://doi.org/10.1103/PhysRevPhysEducRes.12.020110.
5. Karyn L. Lewis et al., "Fitting In to Move Forward: Belonging, Gender, and Persistence in the Physical Sciences, Technology, Engineering, and Mathematics (pSTEM)," *Psychology of Women Quarterly* 41, no. 4 (December 2017): 420–36, https://doi.org/10.1177/0361684317720186.
6. Jessie Brown and Martin Kurzweil, "Instructional Quality, Student Outcomes, and Institutional Finances" (American Council on Education, 2017).
7. Ann E. Austin et al., "Organization Change Networks (OCNs): An Emerging Framework for Understanding Their Development and Functioning," *Innovative Higher Education* (October 28, 2024), https://doi.org/10.1007/s10755-024-09750-4; Anthony S. Bryk et al., *Learning to Improve: How America's Schools Can Get Better at Getting Better* (Harvard Education Press, 2015); Adrianna Kezar and Sean Gehrke, "Communities of Transformation and Their Work Scaling STEM Reform" (University of Southern California, Pullias Center for Higher Education, 2015).
8. AAU (Association of American Universities), "AAU Undergraduate STEM Education Initiative," n.d., https://stemedhub.org/groups/aau; Michael Dennin et al., "Aligning Practice to Policies: Changing the Culture to Recognize and Reward Teaching at Research Universities" (Association of American Universities/Research Corporation for Scientific Advancement, December 2017), https://www.aau.edu/sites/default/files/AAU-Files/STEM-Education-Initiative/Aligning-Practice-To-Policies-Digital.pdf.
9. Roundtable on Systemic Change in Undergraduate STEM Education, Division of Behavioral and Social Sciences and Education, and National Academies of Sciences, Engineering, and Medicine, *Recognizing and Evaluating Science Teaching in Higher Education: Proceedings of a Workshop in Brief*, ed. Susan J. Debad (National Academies Press, 2020), https://doi.org/10.17226/25685.
10. Policy and Global Affairs and National Academies of Sciences, Engineering, and Medicine, *Promotion, Tenure, and Advancement Through the Lens of 2020: Proceedings of a Workshop—In Brief*, ed. Maria Lund Dahlberg and Joe Alper (National Academies Press, 2022), https://doi.org/10.17226/26405.
11. Susan Elrod, Lorne Whitehead, and Mary Taylor Huber, "The Scholarship of Mission: A New Concept for Promoting Scholarly Work Advancing Institutional Goals," *Change: The Magazine of Higher Learning* 52, no. 1 (January 2, 2020): 15–22, https://doi.org/10.1080/00091383.2020.1693815.

12. Boyer 2030 Commission, "The Equity-Excellence Imperative"; Nicky Agate et al., "The Transformative Power of Values-Enacted Scholarship," *Humanities and Social Sciences Communications* 7, no. 1 (December 7, 2020): 165, https://doi.org/10.1057/s41599-020-00647-z.
13. Fay Patel and Hayley M. Lynch, "Glocalization as an Alternative to Internationalization in Higher Education: Embedding Positive Glocal Learning Perspectives," *International Journal of Teaching and Learning in Higher Education* 25 (2013): 223–30; Roland Robertson, "Glocalization: Time-Space and Homogeneity-Heterogeneity," in *Global Modernities*, by Mike Featherstone, Scott Lash, and Roland Robertson (SAGE, 1995), 25–44, https://doi.org/10.4135/9781446250563.n2.

ABOUT THE AUTHORS

ANN E. AUSTIN is a University Distinguished Professor of Higher, Adult, and Lifelong Education at Michigan State University (MSU). She has served in various institutional leadership roles, including as interim dean of the College of Education, interim vice provost for faculty and academic staff affairs, and assistant provost for faculty development. Her research concerns organizational change in higher education, academic work and professional development, equity and inclusion in academic workplaces, teaching and learning issues, doctoral education, and STEM education. She has been a program director at the National Science Foundation (NSF) (2015–2016), a US Fulbright Fellow (1998, South Africa), and president of the Association for the Study of Higher Education (ASHE) (2000–2001), and she is a fellow of the American Educational Research Association (AERA). From 2017 to 2025, she served as cochair of the National Academy of Sciences' Roundtable on Systemic Change in Undergraduate STEM Education.

NOAH D. FINKELSTEIN is a professor and vice chair (2021–2022, 2024–2025) in the department of physics at the University of Colorado Boulder. He conducts research in physics education, specifically studying the conditions that support students' identities, engagement, and outcomes in physics—developing models of context. In parallel, he conducts research on how educational transformations get taken up, spread, and sustained. He is a PI in the Physics Education Research (PER) group and was founding codirector of CU's Center for STEM Learning. He codirects the national Network of STEM Education Centers, is building the STEM DBER-Alliance, and coalitions advancing undergraduate education transformation. He is involved in education policy serving on many national boards, sits on a National Academies' Board on Science Education, is a trustee of the Higher Learning Commission, is a fellow of both the American Physical Society and the American Association for the Advancement of Science, and a Presidential Teaching Scholar and the inaugural Timmerhaus Teaching Ambassador for the University of Colorado system.

ANDREA "DEA" FOLLMER GREENHOOT is a professor of psychology, director of the Center for Teaching Excellence, and Gautt Teaching Scholar at the University of Kansas. Her research focuses on memory and cognitive development, and on strategies for systemic improvement of higher education, informed by cognitive and developmental science. Recent work has examined interventions for enhancing student learning and development, for using assessment data to improve teaching and learning, for representing and evaluating teaching, and for scaling these activities to produce widespread change. She has also been director of the Bay View Alliance (BVA) (2021–2025), a consortium of US and Canadian research universities that collaborate on educational improvement initiatives, and she sits on the National Academies' Roundtable for Systemic Change in Undergraduate STEM Education.

DOUG WARD is associate director of the Center for Teaching Excellence and an associate professor of journalism and mass communications at the University of Kansas. He specializes in helping faculty with generative artificial intelligence, online and hybrid teaching, course transformation, the evaluation of teaching, and the use of technology. He writes frequently about teaching, learning, and the future of higher education, and is the author of *A New Brand of Business* (Temple University Press, 2010).

GABRIELA CORNEJO WEAVER is assistant vice president for academic affairs and research for the University of Massachusetts system and professor of chemistry at UMass Amherst, where she previously served as vice provost for faculty development and the director of the center for teaching and learning. She is an elected fellow of the American Association for the Advancement of Science for distinguished contributions to transforming science education at the undergraduate level. Prior to UMass, she served on the faculty at Purdue University as professor of chemistry and science education and the Jerry and Rosie Semler Director of the Discovery Learning Research Center. She holds a PhD in Chemical Physics from the University of Colorado Boulder.

INDEX